FENG SHUI *for* HOMEBUYERS
EXTERIOR

Feng Shui for Homebuyers - Exterior

The author can be reached at:

Mastery Academy of Chinese Metaphysics Sdn. Bhd. (611143-A)
19-3, The Boulevard, Mid Valley City,
59200 Kuala Lumpur, Malaysia.
Tel   : +603-2284 8080
Fax   : +603-2284 1218
Email   : info@masteryacademy.com
Website: www.masteryacademy.com

DISCLAIMER:

Published by JY Books Sdn. Bhd. (659134-T)

INDEX

Preface   vi

Chapter One: 1
Feng Shui and Your Property

Chapter Two: 23
Essential Understanding

Chapter Three: 51
Environment

Chapter Four: 173
The Internal Environment

Chapter Five: 237
What's not Feng Shui - What is not of any
importance when evaluating a property

Chapter Six: 253
How to Screen a House

Preface

Feng Shui is experiencing something of a renaissance in the 21st century. As a practitioner of this classical Chinese science, I am happy to see that there are so many people interested in finding out how they can tap into the beneficial Qi of the environment to improve their lives, achieve their goals and live well. Unfortunately, the popularity of Feng Shui has also eroded its true identity. Now, everything seems to have a Feng Shui significance, from figurines to crystals to even what colour you dye your hair.

Feng Shui is part of the Chinese Five Arts, and falls under the category of physiognomy. This is in essence, the science of observation, specifically observation of Qi. Hence, classical Feng Shui entails not just the application of formulas through methods such as Flying Stars, Eight Mansions and Xuan Kong Da Gua, but the observation of the environment in which a person lives and works. The study of the environment and the landforms in the environment is sometimes called Forms. I prefer to use its classical name, which is Luan Tou Feng Shui, which loosely translates into 'the face of the mountain'. Unfortunately, there is little reference to landform in many modern books about Feng Shui. Most modern books are about trinkets and figurines. Honestly, this is not what classical Feng Shui is about.

Hence, this book, Feng Shui for Homebuyers is born. I have written this book for several reasons. Firstly, it is to expose Feng Shui enthusiasts and lay persons to the study of urban landforms in a simple and practical manner and increase awareness of Feng Shui as more than just trinkets and figurines. Secondly, I do realise that there are a lot of people who would like to incorporate basic Feng Shui either into their offices or homes in some way, but do not have the inclination to take a formal class. This book is designed to enable simple and basic incorporation of Feng Shui principles, specifically those based on landform and the external environment, into your property.

Thirdly, I realise that often when people are searching for a property to purchase, either for investment or for their own use, they usually have a few choices in mind. Hence, this book has been written to enable the screening of properties, utilising what I call 'Feng Shui Vision'. The idea here is to enable and empower homebuyers to screen out properties that would not generally have good Feng Shui, using the guidelines and principles in this book. To ensure this book achieves the purpose, I have included an illustration or a photograph of each of the principles and guidelines elaborated upon.

If you are inclined to have your property assessed by a professional Feng Shui consultant, this book will enable you to reduce the number of consultations you will need (and save money!) because you will be able to narrow down the number of properties that need to be audited by the consultant. If you have made use of the information in this book well, then not only will you be able to procure a property that has minimal or few problems, Feng Shui wise, but it will make the work of the consultant a lot easier. Why? Because he can then just focus on making the property better instead of trying to figure how to fix it, before making it better. There's no point in wasting money on a consultation if the property doesn't pass muster in the first place.

Remember the goal is to find a place with good basic Feng Shui to begin with. Once you have good basics in place, a consultation, should you be inclined towards one, will be to improve or fine-tune the Feng Shui and to improve the receipt and circulation of Qi from the environment.

And should you not be inclined to a consultation, then the basics in this book will ensure that at the very least, you own and will live in a property that does not have bad Feng Shui. Either way, I hope you will find this book helpful in guiding you towards finding the right property.

Happy House Hunting !

Warmest Regards,

Joey Yap
February 2006

Author's personal website: www.joeyyap.com
Academy website: www.masteryacademy.com | www.masteryjournal.com

MASTERY ACADEMY
OF CHINESE METAPHYSICS™

At www.masteryacademy.com, you will find some useful tools to ascertain key information about the Feng Shui of a property or for study of Astrology.

The Joey Yap Flying Star Calculator can be utilized to plot your home or office Flying Star chart. To find out your personal best directions, use the 8 Mansions Calculator. To learn more about your personal Destiny, you can use the Joey Yap BaZi Ming Pan Calculator to plot your Four Pillars of Destiny – you just need to have your date of birth (day, month, year) and time of birth.

For more information about BaZi, Xuan Kong or Flying Star Feng Shui, or if you wish to learn more about these subjects with Joey Yap, logon to the Mastery Academy of Chinese Metaphysics website at **www.masteryacademy.com**

Chapter One:
Feng Shui and
Your Property

Picture this. You have found the property of your dreams. After much searching and house hunting, you finally find a place that you believe you can call your own. After all the documents are duly signed and you've moved in, you decide to have the property audited by a Feng Shui consultant, since you are planning to undertake renovations anyway. You then discover, to your horror, that the property has a major Feng Shui flaw, which will require not just renovations, but major renovations.

Or how about this scenario – you are at a property development launch and are considering buying one of the properties offered. But then you're unsure which lot to pick for better Feng Shui. How do you decide which phase is more favourable without the help of a Feng Shui consultant?

Perhaps you are a house-hunter on a budget and you find yourself left with the choice of a house that faces a T-junction or perhaps, is close to an electric pylon. You are not superstitious, nor are you a believer in Feng Shui, but you can't help but wonder if it's a good idea to buy the house.

That is the whole point of this book. To help you, the Feng Shui conscious house buyer, pick a property that has positive Feng Shui Quotient (FSQ). To help you screen properties so that you can select a property that will bring benefits and improvement to your quality of life, rather than one that causes you problems.

What if you are a sceptic? Many people will say they do not believe in Feng Shui but yet, would hesitate to buy a property directly facing a T-junction. People also seem to instinctively gravitate away from properties close to electric pylons. They say they don't believe in Feng Shui.

Feng Shui, truth be told, has gotten itself a bit of a bad rep. It is unfortunate that it is often thought of as superstition (no thanks to the proliferation of cultural superstitions and art items being passed off as Feng Shui) - who wants to admit they bought a house based on superstition?

FENG SHUI FOR HOMEBUYERS - EXTERIOR

2

These days Feng Shui is so commercialised that the first impression people have about Feng Shui is that it's all about making money. Again, who wants to admit they bought a house so they can become rich? It's just so crass. Or about placing doohickeys and figurines in all corners of the home – who wants to live in a house that looks like a low class Chinese restaurant?

I have dealt with the real purpose of Feng Shui in my many articles and books so let's not flog a dead horse any more.

But I will say one thing: view Feng Shui as something that supports the creation of a comfortable and happy place to live in and come home to. Feng Shui is all about making your home or property a comfortable and joyous place to live in. Now honestly no one is going to think worse of you or even think you're superstitious, if you tell them you bought your property or built your property to make it comfortable, peaceful and joyous!

There are very few people in this world who would not want to live in a home that is a comfortable, happy, joyous and vibrant . A man's home is his castle as the old saying goes. Feng Shui subscribes to this viewpoint: your home should protect you, nurture you, and be a sanctuary where you can rest and rejuvenate (before going out to conquer the world!).

And truly, that is what Feng Shui is about. Not about making the billionaires, but about creating a comfortable, harmonious and stable living environment first and foremost. Then it is about supporting your goals and aspirations in life. So if you are a skeptic, I urge you to reconsider looking at Feng Shui as superstition or something religious in nature, and instead, see it as a science that is aimed at making your life better by creating a comfortable, positive living and working environment.

FENG SHUI FOR HOMEBUYERS - EXTERIOR

Feng Shui Is An Objective Driven Science

Feng Shui is about harnessing the Qi (energy) of your living environment to help you achieve your goals. Feng Shui is not just about turning your home into a magnet for wealth – it is about making your home, the place that you spend most of your non-working hours in, a comfortable and joyous place to reside in, and of  course, support your life goals. It is about harnessing the Qi or natural energy of your living environment, with a view to helping you achieve your goals in life.

Of course, it helps if you have a goal in life or an objective you wish to achieve. Feng Shui is a goal-orientated science and so that is why the Feng Shui practitioner will first inquire as to what your purpose for getting a consultation is. Before you say, of course, wealth and money, bear in mind that wealth is but just one of the aspects that Feng Shui can assist with. In any case, wealth is not an easy thing to define. It's like asking someone, how rich is rich enough?

In reality, Feng Shui begins with creating a healing home – a place where the Qi flow is pleasant, sentimental and harmonious. A good Feng Shui home is one where the occupants have vibrant health. When it comes to a residential property, Feng Shui practitioners usually put a premium on people luck – ensuring harmony in the family and home and good health.

Once you have health, then you can move on to wealth! But
even then, you need to understand that Wealth Luck in the
study of Feng Shui does not mean that pots of money and
gold will drop from the sky into your backyard once you have
Feng Shui'ed your house. Rather, what it really means is that
the opportunities to make money increase. Career prospects
will improve and business opportunities increase rather than
decrease. The individual must still, however, seize these
opportunities through his own efforts.

A Feng Shui Consultation as an Investment

Even for those who subscribe to the science of Feng Shui, there is a large measure of reluctance to actually get a consultation. Sometimes it is the expense, sometimes it is the hassle, but sometimes it is also the fear of hearing bad news or even, the cost of renovation and the consultation.

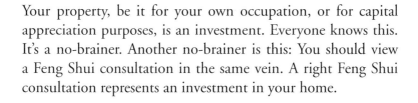

Part of my role as a Feng Shui consultant is helping people understand what a consultation is all about and what value it offers you.

Your property, be it for your own occupation, or for capital appreciation purposes, is an investment. Everyone knows this. It's a no-brainer. Another no-brainer is this: You should view a Feng Shui consultation in the same vein. A right Feng Shui consultation represents an investment in your home.

Here's a trade secret: Implementing Feng Shui in your life does not have to cost an arm and a leg and this book teaches you one of the best techniques for minimising the cost of implementing Feng Shui in your life: just avoid the houses with negative features!

Yes, it is that easy.

You see, this book is meant to help you screen properties so that the cost of a consultation is minimised to just one property. And if you have made good use of the information in this book, and selected a good environment, then you have certainly made the work of the Feng Shui consultant a lot easier. With fewer matters to correct or for that matter, adjust, the cost of implementing Feng Shui in your home will not be as high as well.

Having said that, just as you wouldn't skimp on the furniture or fittings in your home, so a consult isn't something you should skimp on. Now, I'm not saying you need to pay through your nose or renovate your house topsy turvy. But at the same time, please recognize that a fifty dollar consult is exactly that, a fifty dollar consult.

Making use of Feng Shui need not be expensive. But at the same time, please remember, rock bottom bargain basement consultations may not be much help either.

The many faces of Feng Shui

You will notice as you make your way through this book that there are no 'products' suggested. The product-driven approach is not a part of Classical Feng Shui but is more what I call 'New Age Feng Shui' or 'Pop Feng Shui'. I also do not make any recommendations about decoration or colours for the same reason.

Classical Feng Shui, of which the methods and techniques in this book are based on, is about understanding Qi flow and how that Qi flow affects your property. A good part of this understanding comes from being able to evaluate the landform and environmental features that surround a property. The techniques and methods I will rely on in this book are aimed at showing you how to harness the Qi, by identifying good Qi-collecting features in a property and how to avoid Sha Qi (negative energies). By identifying negative environmental features and choosing not to buy a house or property with such features, you are already taking a positive step towards getting a property with good Feng Shui. Remember, the name of the game is not to try to fix something that is broken, but to get something that is good in itself, so you can improve on it!

Yet even in Classical Feng Shui, there are many systems, with different concepts, some which even seem downright contradictory.

There is the San Yuan 三元 system, which is about the time cycle of luck and how the time factor influences the quality of Qi in an area, or the San He 三合 system which looks at environmental influences such as mountains and rivers. You may have also heard of Xuan Kong Da Gua 玄空大卦, a system for fine-tuning of the house's Qi point to match the internal lay out with the external lay out and to ensure the correct landform is in the correct palace.

Xuan Kong Da Gua is based on very specific time measurements and time selection, from when to place a remedy and when to install something to very precise solutions for dealing with exceptions to the rules. For example, if a principle states a property should have no water in the Northeast in general, Da Gua prescribes a small area in the Northeast, such as 2.5 degrees, where there is an exception to the rule. Xuan Kong Da Gua 玄空大卦 requires a proper and thorough understanding of Di Li Bian Zheng 地理辨正, a ancient classic on Xuan Kong Da Gua 玄空大卦.

Most people have heard of the Flying Stars 飛星 system, which is the basic system of determining the potential of each palace and when the potential will be unleashed or how you can unleash it in terms of wealth and people luck. The Flying Stars system enables practitioners to understand what effects a certain sector in the house has on its residents at certain points in time. And then there is Ba Zhai 八宅 or Eight Mansions Feng Shui, which is a more traditional system and utilises the basic static Qi energy map of a house for long-term Feng Shui. It also covers the personal favourable directions, which is not a component of other systems.

These are but a few common 'methods' of Feng Shui most Classical Feng Shui practitioners would advocate. All these systems of Feng Shui often sound intimidating to a beginner. Fret not. This book is not about teaching you a 'formula'. This book contains the 'preliminary' assessment method that is used PRIOR to the application of ANY of the above Feng Shui methods. What does this mean for the average person with little or no Feng Shui knowledge? Essentially, if the property you have in mind does not pass muster when it comes to the simple assessment methods detailed in this book, the property's Feng Shui is at best average, and at worse, dire and there's unlikely to be much improvement to the situation even when the formula-based assessment methods are added to the audit.

The goal of this book is to help you self-assess prospective properties. Hence, a lot of the materials in this book have been condensed, synthesized from various techniques and theories about Landform and written in a manner to make it as easy to understand as possible. But it is important you recognize that this book cannot teach you every technique in Classical Feng Shui or all the concepts and theories. Nor is it designed to enable you to become a consultant in the course of one weekend. It has been strictly written for the purposes of enabling you to screen prospective properties.

How to make use of this book

Let me tell you another little trade secret: before any of the sophisticated formulas in the various systems of Feng Shui are utilised, the environment and landforms or Luan Tou must first be scrutinised. Any good Feng Shui master must and will examine the environment around the property before moving onto the property per se. A Feng Shui assessment without the evaluation of external environmental features is not a thorough Feng Shui audit.

If you find that a prospective property has many of the negative features and forms, as indicated in this book, thus possessing a negative Feng Shui Quotient (FSQ), buying the property then hiring a Feng Shui consultant is wasting your money twice over.

First, you have to buy the place. Then you have to foot out more money just to fix the problems. After that only can you undertake renovations to improve it further. Why buy a property that needs to be fixed, before you can make it better, when you can buy a property that is already good and simply needs to be made better? Better yet, find a place that is already a high quality property, with positive FSQ, in which case, a Feng Shui consult would be icing on the cake.

That is the goal of this book – to help you find a property that is already in itself fairly good, Feng Shui-wise, with the help of photographs, illustrations and aerial images and with a minimum need to renovate or undertake big modifications to the property.

By evaluating the environmental aspect yourself, through a bit of legwork and homework with this book, you are ensuring that any prospective property that you have Feng Shui'ed is at least rectifiable or improveable using the formulas.

Bottom line: Qi collection

Why is landform so important and why are simple and seemingly innocuous objects like lamp posts and sharp roofs such bad guys?

First thing to note is that there are two types of Qi that can be found in the environment: Sha Qi 煞氣 and Sheng Qi 生氣. Of course, we want to not only have Sheng Qi in our environment but also be able to collect and distribute the Sheng Qi in our property. Similarly, we don't like to have Sha Qi in the environment or in any of the sectors of the property if possible.

The second point to understand is the concept of Feng Shui, at its most basic. The idea of Feng Shui is very aptly summed up in the saying Cang Feng Ju Qi 藏風聚氣 – this means to stall the wind, and collect the Qi. If you go to the place where there's a very strong gusting wind, the place cannot be good. This is because places with very strong wind cannot collect Qi. In the Book of Burial, it says: "Qi is dispersed by the wind, and gathers at the boundaries of water" (乘風則散，界水則止).

If a place is too open or spacious, then Qi cannot collect. If there is an obstruction, then Qi is being blocked. What about sharp roofs and sharp angles then? It is not that the sharply angled roof tiles are 'shooting' Qi at your house. Rather, when the wind hits the sharp roof that points at your house or door, it focuses and directs the wind at your home. That sector of your home, which is hit by the wind, then cannot collect Qi. It instead becomes afflicted by Sha Qi or negative Qi.

乘風則散，界水則止

14

Good news! This book is Formula Free!

Yes, you read it right. This book is free of complex Feng Shui formulas. Formula calculations are substantial part of a Feng Shui consultation but this is best left to the consultant. You do not need to know Feng Shui formulas like Five Ghost Carry Treasure 五鬼運財, Dragon Gate Eight Formations 龍門八局 and Assistant Star Transformation Method to effectively screen houses.

Remember, the true trade secret of a Feng Shui Master is always the environment first. In the old days, mansions and homes of noblemen and imperial officials were mostly selected using very basic landform observations techniques. So don't under-estimate the power of simple techniques and ordinary observations.

Accordingly, it is perfectly safe for you to undertake a preliminary evaluation of the property just based on forms, both for the interior and exterior. Yes, even the interior of a property can have landform.

In any case, it just makes more sense. Most people can perceive a mountain, or a river, or make out the shape of a building and determine if something is sharp or not. It doesn't take a lot to learn if something is pointing at your Main Door. But learning formulas requires time and indeed, a lot of basic knowledge and understanding. Since this is a book for people who have little or no Feng Shui background, putting in formulas just adds to the intimidation. I am a firm believer in making things simple and uncomplicated, which is why this book has no formulas!

Finally, there is an old saying in the ancient classics: "There are no fake forms and there are no real formulas". (Luan Tou Wu Jia, Li Qi Wu Zhen 巒頭無假, 理氣無眞). What does this mean? Essentially, it means that what is in the environment, the landform, must always be considered, before any formulas are applied. So in looking at landform or Luan Tou first, you are already taking an important step towards checking your Feng Shui the way a professional Classical Feng Shui consultant would.

Caveat: Have Realistic Expectations

You need to recognize that good locations with 100% positive FSQ are few and far between and not easy to find. Also, purchasing any ready-made property instantly comes with certain limitations. In an ideal situation, finding your own land and then constructing your property on it, in accordance with Feng Shui principles, is best. But of course, this is not a realistic option, at least financially, for many people. And even if you can afford to buy a piece of land, finding good land is difficult and honestly, not something every person can do these days, although it is not impossible. And it is not something the layperson can do with ease – you need to at least be intimately familiar with Ru Di Yan 入地眼 or Entering Earth Eye Classics, a San He text on landform.

But never, as I always tell my students, let what you can't do, stop you from what you can do. And this book should help you do that. If you have the opportunity and the means to purchase your own land, use this book to screen and eliminate the unsuitable options with negative FSQ. Then get a professional Feng Shui Master to survey the best two or three choices. This way, your final three options are unlikely to be bad quality land, Feng Shui-wise, and your Feng Shui Master is really just helping you pick the best of three good options.

If you are purchasing a newly-built house, this book will help you, at the very least, determine which lot to pick and which ones to avoid, or even, which housing estate to select, based on surrounding environmental features in the township or area. I have included lots of pictures in this book to help you get a visual perspective on landform and the environmental features frequently found within an urban landscape. Worst case scenario, you will know what questions to ask the property developer when you view a prospective property development.

For those who are purchasing ready built properties within an established neighbourhood, you will be able to screen houses using the tips in this book and at least ensure that you buy a house with minimum problems at some measure of positive FSQ. As it is the trend these days for people to buy old houses and then renovate them to suit their needs, this book will also help you find a property that is favourable to begin with, so that your renovations can then be used to fine-tune the Feng Shui to suit your goals and needs.

Remember The Role of Heaven

Of course, at the end of the day, one must not forget that ultimately, one must consider the 'Heaven' aspect or a person's destiny, which is analysed through Purple Star 紫微 astrology or BaZi 八字 astrology. The element of Heaven Luck must be given consideration because ultimately, the universe, according to Chinese Metaphysics, involves the interplay of Heaven, Earth and Man. Heaven being Destiny, Earth being Feng Shui and Man being one's own actions.

Tian
Heaven

Di
Earth

If it is not destined to be yours, you are unlikely to have it. You may be able to find the perfect land, but perhaps it is not for sale or you can't afford it. Or you have the perfect land but you don't have the right Feng Shui formulas or methodologies to

Ren
Man

tap into it. The key issue about the Heaven Luck component is to remember that Heaven Luck also has some impact on your ability to find a good place to live.

Finally, it is also important to know that in a proper Feng Shui consult, the Heaven Luck of the occupants must be considered as well because if a person's problems are not ascertained through analysing his destiny, then Feng Shui cannot be properly applied to ensure his life goals are achieved or fostered through the Qi in the environment.

Remember, Feng Shui is the prescription, Destiny Analysis affords the diagnosis. You can't have prescription without diagnosis.

Feng Shui is not paranoia

Along with being realistic in your expectations, you should also not be terrified into inaction. Sometimes, the effects of the environment are important, sometimes they are not because certain occupants are not so affected by that environmental feature. Also, environmental features are about immediacy. What is closest to you and nearest to you is what matters, not what is miles away! It is also important to think about how a certain environmental feature impacts your house, if at all, and which occupant it affects, instead of just being fixated on the presence of a negative feature.

If there is a sharp object in front of your property but it is very far from your property, why should you care? The ancient texts say, if the distance between the Sha Qi and your property is a distance of 1,000 horses , there is no effect. This is not an exact distance and don't take it literally – the idea is for us to appreciate that you do not have to be obsessed with everything pointy and sharp around you. In this day and age, it is impossible to escape anything pointy and sharp unless you want to live without electricity or cable TV.

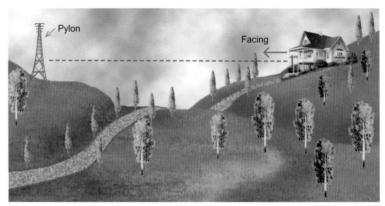

Not every sharp object is a cause for concern - the question is, how far away is it from your property?

Similarly, if the negative feature affects say, a person who is Dui Gua (兌卦). One of the interpretations of Dui Gua is young girl. Now, if none of the occupants in the property is a young girl, then you do not have a problem with that house!

A little common sense is good when you are making use of this book. Remember, it is not easy to find a place which has none of the bad, and all of the good. So you should be realistic in your expectations and practical. Not having 3 out of 5 of the negative features is already a pretty good situation. Having a minor negative feature that can easily be rectified through simple renovations or placing of a screen or water, is also an acceptable situation.

The key is to prioritise – you should be more concerned with what is at your doorstep, rather than what is 50km away from you. Just as what is immediately affecting your Main Door is more important than what points at the side of your house.

Finally, remember that before any Feng Shui master can make use of any formulas, the environment must first be examined. So by doing this aspect yourself, you are ensuring that any prospective property that you have Feng Shui'ed at least, is rectifiable using the formulas or improve-able using the formulas. If you find that your property has many of the negative features mentioned in this book, hiring a Feng Shui master is wasting your money. First, you have to spend a lot of money to fix the problem and secondly, why buy a place that needs to be fixed, before you can make it better, when you can buy a place that is already good and simply needs to be made better? Find a place that is already a high quality property, and let the Feng Shui consult be icing on the cake.

Chapter Two: Essential Understanding

Now that you understand how this book can be used, you need to have a little bit of basic knowledge. I promised this book would be formula free so there won't be any complicated calculations in this section. Instead, this section will explain the basic tools you will need to screen houses and elaborate on how to obtain the references you need to have in order to make use of the information in the subsequent chapters.

I'll delve into some of the key basics. For example you'll need to understand what is Qi and how you make use of a basic tool like a scout's compass to obtain the Facing of a property. It is the bare minimum of information that you will need to know and understand in order to make the best use of the information contained in this book.

That Qi Word

Qi is the core of Feng Shui, indeed, the whole point of Feng Shui. People are often surprised at how simple the concept of Feng Shui is: find the Qi, and collect it. That is what Feng Shui is all about essentially.

What is Qi people often ask? It is the natural energy that is found in the environment. One thing to remember about Qi is that we are interested in what is natural, not man-made. Now, because we live in a civilised world with buildings and modern conveniences, Feng Shui has evolved to take into account how structures like skyscrapers and highways affect a property. But evolution should never be taken to extreme. Today, there is often a belief that anything under the sun, from cactus to your hair colour, affects your Qi. No it doesn't. Real Qi is natural, not man-made. Real Qi emanates from the natural mountains and water on our planet, not something you buy or have built in your back yard.

In Classical Feng Shui, we are mainly concerned with where the Qi is, what kind of Qi you have in the area and of course, how to bring it to the property, retain it, and distribute it throughout the home or property. The Feng Shui consultant's job is to evaluate the landform in the area, find out what Qi is present and then design or make use of formulas and the property, to tap, collect and distribute the Qi. This is what Feng Shui consultants mean when they talk about "harnessing Qi in the environment".

When Qi flows, the occupants of a property are healthier, more vibrant and perform better, hence contributing to their wealth and ability to capitalise on opportunities. When beneficial Qi is clogged, or when Qi does not reach a property, then the well-being of the occupants is affected, which in turn affects their work performance, relationships with those around them and their capacity to function at their best. When people are unhappy or sick, they don't perform at their optimum and don't see opportunities coming their way.

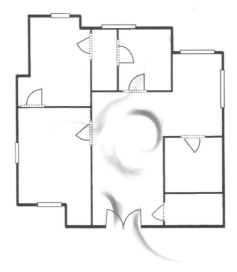

In this book, we will be looking at basic landform concepts and principles and I will be talking about how landform can be used to block, re-direct, repel or collect Qi, depending on whether it is negative killing Qi or good, positive benevolent Qi.

When it comes to Qi, the main thing you need to understand is Qi is either positive (meaning it is growing, benevolent, sentimental and harmonious), which is known in Feng Shui terminology as Sheng Qi 生氣 (Growing Qi) or it is merciless, dead, stagnant, killing or clogged, in Feng Shui terminology, it is called Sha Qi 煞氣 (Killing Qi).

Know the Geography

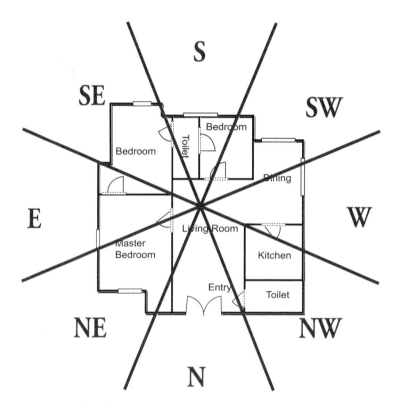

Okay, now that you understand what Qi is, let's move on to the next little skill you will need. To make full use of this book, some simple map reading ability and also, a basic knowledge of the cardinal directions is needed. Now, it's nothing too complicated. First, you need to be able to identify the 8 cardinal directions – North, South, East, West, Northeast, Northwest, Southeast, Southwest – with reference to the property you are assessing. Remember, each property may have a different orientation so you need to be able to identify these directions in accordance with the property you are evaluating.

Getting the directions is quite easy – you can use a simple scout's compass and I'll explain later on, where you should stand to take the direction. Seeing as we are now in the electronic age, there are also some electronic compasses that are quite useful and handy and make it easier to ascertain the directions because they take out the problem of shaky hands. If you want to be a little bit more sophisticated, you can buy a Feng Shui Luo Pan but this necessitates learning how to use it so a compass is more suitable for most people. I do recommend that you get a compass that is reliable and accurate, and if you have difficulty finding one, you may purchase a Mini Feng Shui Compass that I have produced for this purpose.

Joey Yap's Mini Feng Shui Compass

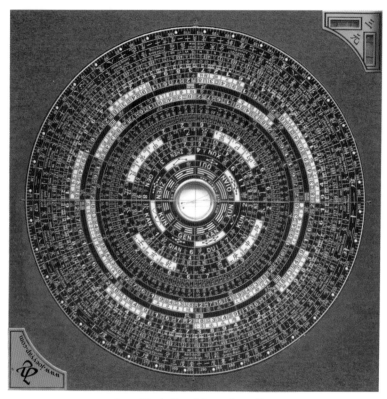

Joey Yap's San Yuan Luo Pan

Why do you need to know directions? Well, firstly, it gives you information on where the problem will arise and how it will arise and sometimes, you can even determine when it will arise. If for example, you have Sha Qi in the West, based on the Trigrams, you will know this affects the youngest daughter in the house but you don't have a youngest daughter, then the property is fine.

How to Take a Direction

The first step in taking a direction is to observe the façade of the property. How do you decide what the façade is? The main technique is to observe the direction the house was designed to face. The common mistake when it comes to taking a direction that many people make is to assume that they have to use the Main Door as the reference point. Sometimes, the Main Door is the façade, sometimes it is not. So to be on the safe side, look at the façade.

Door Facing + House Facing (Facade)

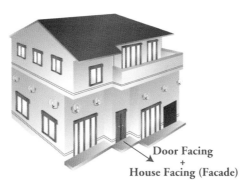

**Door Facing
+
House Facing (Facade)**

The door facing and the house facing are the same direction.

ESSENTIAL UNDERSTANDING

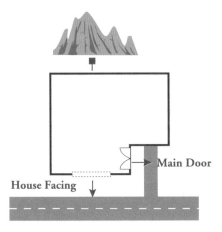

The door facing and the house facing in this example are not the same direction. In such cases, you always base the facing direction on the direction the house faces, not the door.

Once you have identified where the building faces (known as the Facing), stand at the Central Palace (that's Feng Shui terminology for the center of the façade) look out and see what direction the compass yields. That direction gives you the Facing Direction of the property.

Looking outwards

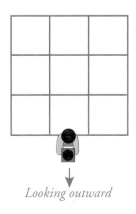

Looking outward

The next step, after you have obtained the Facing Direction of the property, is to demarcate the directions and then the palaces. The demarcation of the directions is for exterior Feng Shui, 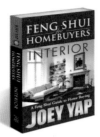 which is the focus of this book. The demarcation of the palaces is for interior Feng Shui, which is covered in depth in Feng Shui for Homebuyers - Interiors. The demarcation of the direction is done using the 8-Pie Method whilst the demarcation of the palaces or internal sectors is done using the 9 Palaces or 9 Grids method.

Demarcating the directions is done with the 8-Pie Method. We use the 8-Pie Method for the external demarcation because there is no central palace or sector, only a central spot. The diagram below shows you how to demarcate the directions using the 8-Pie Method.

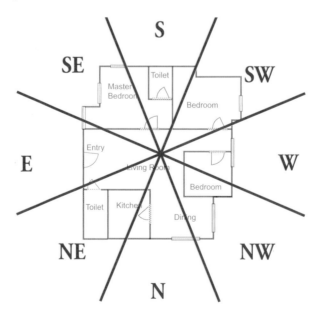

The 8-Pie Method

When we are referencing the internal environment of the home, the impact is evaluated based on the 9 Palaces. The 9 Palaces are used for the interior because Qi does not move by borderlines – Qi moves by room size as it can fill a room or contract in a space. My books on Eight Mansions and Flying Stars, and Feng Shui for Homebuyers - Interior will focus more on the 9 Palaces because that is related to interior Feng Shui. In this book, we will mainly be looking at the external environment so the 8 directions are our main concern.

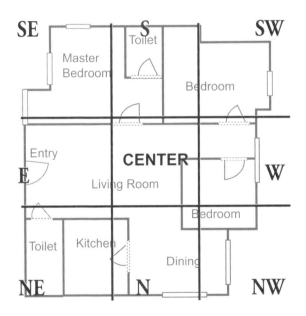

The 9 palaces method

Demarcating the Directions

To demarcate the 8 directions, you need to first have a plan of the property. Preferably, use the architects plan as this will give you a more accurate plan. To make it easy for you to demarcate your home using the 8-Pie Method, a simple stencil is included on page 37. Photocopy this image onto a transparency and then use it to demarcate the 8 Directions on your property.

This book only requires you to have the basic 8 cardinal directions and so I will not go into the 24 Mountains or the 64 Hexagrams. The 24 Mountains and the 64 Hexagrams are utilised at a professional level for directions. As this book is only meant to be a guidebook, I will keep it at a simple level.

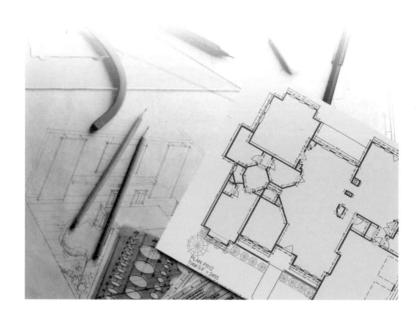

Place the stencil over your house plan, with the central point matching the central point of your house plan. Turn it until you get the exact degree of the property's Facing Direction. So for example, if your property faces North at 5 degrees, you will draw the 8-Pies as below.

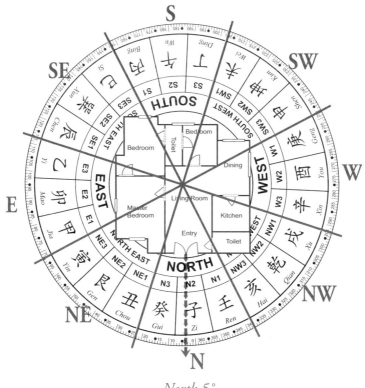

North 5°

If your property faces N3 at 15° degrees, you will draw the 8-Pies as below.

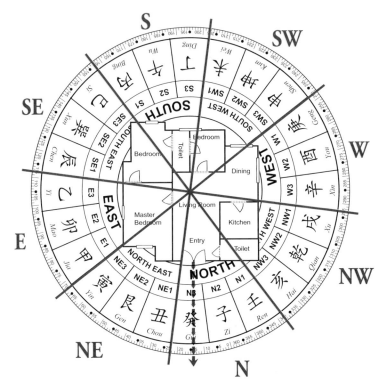

Facing N3 at 15°

Extend out the 8-Pie direction lines a little further than the borders of the property so you can also use it to identify and mark any external environmental features on the plan. Label the sectors North, South, East, West, Northeast, Northwest, Southeast, Southwest. Now you will be able to know which sector belongs to which direction.

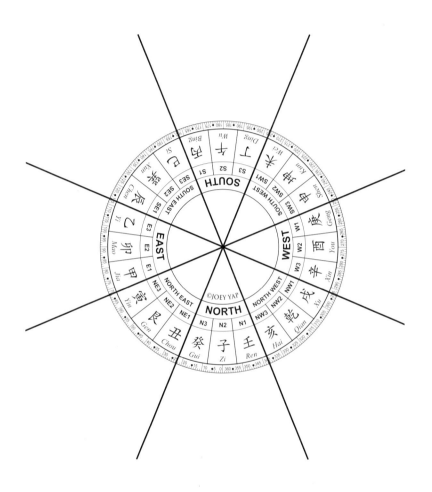

The Trigrams

Each direction and sector has a corresponding trigram, based on the Ba Gua. Each trigram in turn, has a significance and a meaning. Now, these meanings can run into the thousands, but I have included a basic list for you here.

Qian 乾 ☰

Element:	Metal.
Number:	6
Direction:	Northwest
People:	The emperor, father, adult, old people, senior person, famous person, emperor's servant, government officer and civil servants, boss, leader, chairman.
Body Parts:	Head, bone, lung.
Sickness:	Head/Brain related disease, lung disease, muscle and bone disease.
Color:	Gold, silver, white.

Kun 坤 ☷

Element:	Earth.
Number:	2
Direction:	Southwest
People:	Mother, step-mother, farmer, villager, people/crowd, old lady and people with big bellies/fat people.
Body Parts:	Abdomen, spleen, flesh, stomach.
Sickness:	Abdominal disease, stomach disease, poor appetite, indigestion.
Color:	Yellow, black.

Zhen 震

Element:	Wood.
Number:	3
Direction:	East
People:	Eldest son.
Body Parts:	Foot, liver, hair, voice.
Sickness:	Foot disease, liver disease, worries and shock.
Color:	Dark green and jade green.

Xun 巽

Element:	Wood.
Number:	4
Direction:	Southeast
People:	Eldest daughter, widow.
Body Parts:	Thigh, Qi and disease of Feng/wind/gas.
Sickness:	Thigh problems, disease of Feng/wind, intestinal disease, stroke and disease of Qi.
Color:	Green

Kan 坎 ☵

Element:	Water.
Number:	1
Direction:	North
People:	Middle son, people who are working on the sea/river/lake etc. for example: fisherman, sailor, pirates.
Body Parts:	Ear, blood, kidney.
Sickness:	Ear sickness, infection, kidney and stomach problem, diarrhea.
Color:	Black, blue.

Li 離 ☲

Element:	Fire.
Number:	9
Direction:	South
People:	Middle daughter, writers.
Body Parts:	Eye, heart.
Sickness:	Eye disease, heart disease
Color:	Red, purple.

Gen   艮 ☶

Element:	Earth.
Number:	8
Direction:	Northeast
People:	Youngest son, young kids, people living in the jungle, a hermit or a person who has lots of free time.
Body Parts:	Finger, bone, nose, back, back bone.
Sickness:	Problems of the finger/toes, stomach and back.
Color:	Yellow.

Dui   兑 ☱

Element:	Metal.
Number:	7
Direction:	West
People:	Youngest daughter, mistress, singer, actor.
Body Parts:	Tongue, mouth, throat, lung, phlegm, saliva.
Sickness:	Mouth or tongue disease, throat disease, respiratory disease, lack of appetite.
Color:	White.

How do you use the Trigrams? It's easy.

Let's say you have identified a negative feature in the South section of your property. For example, there is an electric pylon in that direction. South is Li Gua. Li Gua, amongst other things, represents the heart. Let's say there is an electric pylon in the South of your property, and your door is at the South of the property facing the pylon. Now, of course you know that a negative feature exerting negative Sha Qi on the Main Door is not a good thing. But bad or good are what I call 'kindergarten' Feng Shui. You don't just want to know bad or good, you want to know, who or what it affects. That's where the Trigrams come in.

If there is a negative Sha Qi feature in front of the Main Door in the South, the negative effects are most likely heart related or eye related because the Sha Qi is in the South and the South, which is Li Gua , represents the heart or eyes.

Li 離 ☲

Element:	Fire.
Number:	9
Direction:	South
People:	Middle daughter.
Body Parts:	Eye, heart.
Sickness:	Eye disease, heart disease.
Color:	Red, purple.

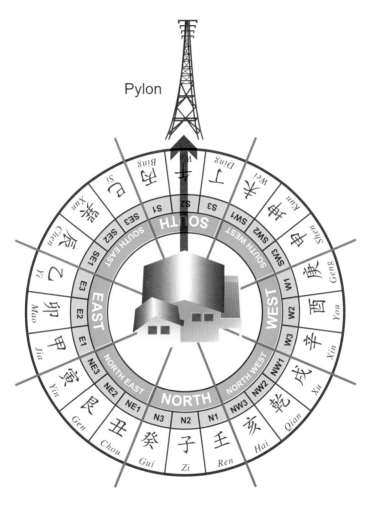

Pylon

Property with South sector main door, facing the pylon

Armed with the information in this book, and knowledge of the Trigrams, you can not only identify negative features and Sha Qi around your home, but also know what problems these features will generally give rise to. So if you cannot remove the negative Sha Qi or change your door, then you can at least take human action – buy more insurance or take care of your health for example.

As the Trigrams provide information on WHO is affected by the negative environmental features and how they are likely to be affected, you are also able to make a more informed decision on the property in question. Remember, in Feng Shui, we don't want to be paranoid. A negative feature in itself is not a problem unless it affects something (a property), someone (an occupant of the property) in some way (health problem, money problem)

Taking the example again of the property with a negative Sha Qi in the South pointing at the Main Door, we know that it will create heart-related or eye-related problems. But which occupant specifically will have a problem? Li Gua relates to middle-aged single women. So for example, if you do not have a middle-aged single woman living in the property, then the negative feature is not an issue.

A thorough analysis by a Feng Shui consultant will of course be able to pinpoint which occupant more specifically. But for the lay person, this will enable you to decide if you should buy

the property or not. If none of the permanent occupants of the house described above are middle aged single women, then there is no issue or problem in the immediate short-term.

Thinking Feng Shui,
Seeing with Feng Shui Vision

The methodology of a Feng Shui audit and what a consultant does is not something I can teach you in a simple book. The principles in the classical text on landform, the Entering Earth Eye (Ru Di Yan 入地眼) classics, really require a person to walk the mountains in China before the principles on landform can be understood and appreciated. But the objective in this section will be to boil down some of the main considerations that almost every qualified professional Feng Shui consultant will be taking into account when they observe the landform in the environment around the property. The two key observations are Mountain and Water and the primary consideration is location.

The first thing you need to do is observe the location of the mountain and water. In the chapter on mountains and water, I will explain to you WHERE you want to see a mountain, and where you want to see water.

Now, Feng Shui, like any other science, is about qualifying your observation. So you should ask yourself, is the mountain a good mountain, or a bad mountain? Is it good water, or bad water that I have in proximity to my property? What about the shape? Is the shape a conducive shape? Or one that makes Qi collection difficult? Forms is about the observation of the Qi in the environment and the landform and also, the method of collecting Qi through suitable Qi containers, such as the land and the building.

How the Feng Shui consultant works

Here's an insight into how a professional Feng Shui consultant would analyse and audit a property. This is not what you are expected to do, but just to give you an idea of the kind of research and homework that a consultant should do.

Usually the consultant will inspect the entire area, up to a 10-15km radius of the area surrounding the property. The consultant will be familiar with the mountains and water in the area. So for example, a truly good Feng Shui master must know what 'dragons' are in Taman Tun Dr. Ismail (a well-known residential township in Kuala Lumpur), what kind of river formations in the vicinity and how it is related to your particular land, even though it is a small piece of land.

A Classical Feng Shui consultant should be able to tell one type of mountain from another

Every piece of land and every area has its own unique environmental influences. Now, it is the job of the Feng Shui consultant to know this.

To know that Mid Valley Megamall, a well-known mall in Malaysia, is not about the Flying Stars but it is about the location of the mountain and water and the study of the formations in the vicinity, not the internal layout alone. To know what kind of Mountain there is in Taman Tun Dr. Ismail. You are not expected to know all these or even to attempt all these for the purposes of this book.

Aerial image of Mid Valley Megamall - a Feng Shui consultant should be able to identify the incoming 'Dragons' and the type of Water in the area, not just the Flying Stars Chart.

So what should you be doing?

So what is practical for the layperson to do? It will be quite safe if you drove around within a 1-2km radius of the house or land of your choice. You should observe the immediate environment and check the mountains and determine the location of water. Now, the greater environment can of course impact on your property but that part of the evaluation, along with looking for the Dragon Veins and understanding the Mountain and Water Formations, should safely be left to a qualified Feng Shui consultant. For the average person, a 1-2km radius survey should suffice.

Once you have checked the immediate environment, you can then look into the more immediate external environment such as your neighbours and negative features close to the property, and of course, evaluate the internal Feng Shui of the property. Remember this golden rule: you only look inside the house once you are satisfied with what is outside the house.

Cure-It Syndrome

I must address a very important misconception that is prevalent amongst the public about Feng Shui cures. It's this: not everything has a cure. And even if something has a cure, not every cure works brilliantly. In fact, in Feng Shui, we prefer not to have to constantly implement cures in a property.

As I have said in chapter 1, why get something that is broken, which you have to fix before you can use it? Why not start with something that is usable in the first place? So, don't be fixated on the notion that something negative should be or must be cured. Focus instead on getting a property or location that is good in itself.

In some instances, where the landform feature is negative but easily rectifiable, then I have indicated how this can be done. However, not every scenario has a cure indicated. This is because some involve highly technical applications, using Water formulas or Xuan Kong Da Gua or Flying Stars calculations, some require proper date selection to complement the implementation of the cure and in some instances, there is no cure. So I do not mention a way to correct the problem. Remember, just like in war, there is no cowardice in a strategic retreat, so in Feng Shui, there is nothing wrong with passing up on a property because it is not right. Don't be afraid to do this.

Chapter Three: Environment

The environment plays an important role in evaluating the Feng Shui of your property. This is because the environment that surrounds your property is what generates and creates Qi. Tapping Qi is what Feng Shui is all about. Hence, environment is a very important factor that we pay attention to during a Feng Shui audit.

If you are new to Feng Shui, you might be wondering what this reference to 'environment' is all about. I am not referring to whether or not there is air pollution or water pollution in the area (although these do have some significance). In Feng Shui, when we talk about the environment, we are talking about the mountains and water in the area.

The environment (mountains, rivers, valleys, roads) play an extremely important role in determining the quality of Qi for your home

Finding a good environment is always the first step towards ensuring your property has good Feng Shui. If your property is located in an area that has a good environment, then the job of your Feng Shui consultant is a lot easier. If your property is located in a bad environment, then the consultant's job is not only harder, but sometimes limited in scope. As the old saying goes, you can't make a silk purse out of a sow's ear. Similarly, if your property doesn't receive good Qi or is located in an area with bad Qi, there's not too much a consultant can do to change that. So, find a good environment and you start off on a positive footing.

Now, I am assuming that you already have identified several options in terms of the property you wish to purchase. So the purpose of this section is to help you evaluate the environment that surrounds each of these options.

This section is divided into 5 sub-sections: land, mountain, water, roads and open spaces. I will cover each of the important aspects of these topics. This is not an exhaustive exploration of the issues relating to Luan Tou 巒頭 or Landform Feng Shui. The true study of Landform Feng Shui can only come by walking the mountains with a Master.

This book is meant to help you use 'Feng Shui Vision' when viewing properties but it is not meant to turn you into a practitioner. So in the spirit of keeping things simple and easy, I have selected the issues which I believe are most relevant to a homebuyer or person looking for a plot of land to purchase for a property and which are also easy to apply practically.

Mountains are formed by the magnetic pull of the earth in relation to the star constellations in the sky in the study of Chinese Metaphysics. Mountains generate Qi in the area and are often referred to in ancient Feng Shui texts as 'Dragons'.

Contrary to popular misconception, Mountains are a Yin environmental feature, and not a Yang environmental feature as many people incorrectly assume. Mountains are regarded as Yin because they do not move. Stillness and quietness represents Yin. Where a Mountain is located in relation to your property is vital in determining the quality of the Qi in your area or if you have any Qi at all. Yin, being 'female' gives birth to 'Qi' in your environment. Thus, good quality mountains are an essential ingredient for superior Feng Shui.

Water – the Qi Carrier

It is said in the ancient classic books, "water is the blood of the Dragon". Mountains are Yin, Water is Yang. Water demarcates and collects the Qi in an area. Accordingly an area with good water placement and formations can foster good convergence and collection of Qi. When it comes to water, we are interested in both the type of water, and its location, where it should be and how it should flow. Water, being 'Yang' fertilises the Yin Qi of the mountain. Thus the converging between Mountain and Water formations is known as the 'dragon spot', an area where positive Qi resides.

Water helps converge Qi in an area

Sometimes an environment will have no water features but there will be roads. Did you know that roads constitute virtual water in Feng Shui? They are also carriers of Qi into or away from a property. Accordingly, when we look at an environment, we must also look at the roads, and where they carry Qi to and how the Qi flows along them.

Open Spaces – Qi Convergence

Open spaces are also important in Feng Shui because this is where Qi can collect or be disperse. In Feng Shui terminology, an open space is usually referred to as the Bright Hall or Ming Tang 明堂. In Feng Shui, we like a broad and spacious Bright Hall where Qi can collect and settle, before it is re-distributed around the property.

Tiananmen Square

An open space in front of a building is called a 'Bright Hall'.

Land - the container of Qi

When we talk about the land in Feng Shui, we are talking about the container of Qi. In Feng Shui, you can only tap and harness whatever Qi your land receives from the external environment. So picking the right kind of land, and land that can receive Qi from the environment, is very important. In the context of Feng Shui, good land is land that can receive and contain the Qi, which you then tap and harness using your building or structure. In essence, your land is like a Qi Tupperware. If you have a good Tupperware (read, good land) then Qi doesn't escape or become stale inside it. If you have a bad Tupperware, then Qi for some reason cannot collect in the land or escapes or leaks out easily.

The building or house on the land is the micro perspective; the land is the macro perspective. Micro depends on the macro. Similarly, the house is the macro perspective when one is looking at interior Feng Shui, with the individual rooms being the micro.

Different types of land size and shape will contain and attract different qualities of Qi from the immediate environment

Shape Matters

The first thing that you must examine is the shape or cut of the land. This is usually easily ascertained by having a professional surveyor survey the land for you, or by obtaining the relevant documents from the developer or the land office. It is usually easier to determine the shape of the land if you are looking from a higher perspective.

Land shapes determine what kind of Qi the land carries but also, how much Qi the land can store or hold. Good Feng Shui masters not only look at shape, but also will look at the soil of the land to determine its quality.

Square-shaped land

Square shapes denote balanced Qi and also represent the Earth element in the study of Five Elements. The Five Elements is an integral concept in Chinese Metaphysics and is one of the core backbone concepts in Feng Shui. In the study of Five Elements, Earth represents stability and security. A home should be a stable, secure home (a home after all, as the saying goes, is a man's castle) and the more stable the land in which the house sits on, the less it is likely to be affected by any negative Qi that occurs as a result of the time influence or any developments in the environment.

A square piece of land also makes it easier to ensure equal proportions of each Gua in the 8 directions and it is easier to achieve a balance in the distribution of Qi within the property. Hence, an Earth element shaped piece of land is the preferred choice when it comes to land shape, be it a big piece of land or a small piece of land. This is why Feng Shui masters usually recommend square shaped land. It is the safest option and it is very hard to go wrong with square shaped land.

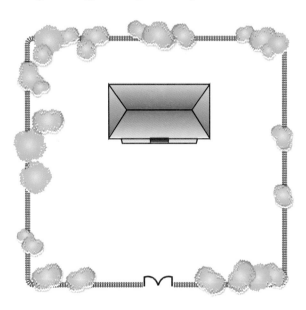

Rectangular-shaped land is the second best option when it comes to selecting land. Although it is not as good as a square shape, it is still considered to be a balanced shape. If you have a choice of rectangular shaped land, it is better to select property that is vertically long or of long length, rather than horizontally long or long in width.

Look at the three types of rectangular land shape in the diagram on the next page. Shape A is preferred over shape B because it is generally better to have long Qi rather than narrow Qi. However, this is not to mean that you should chose a land with a very long length, as in shape C because this then means that while you have long Qi, you also have narrow and tight Qi. The Nine Palaces in the home will accordingly be tightly squeezed and this is not good.

Rectangular-shaped land

Shape A

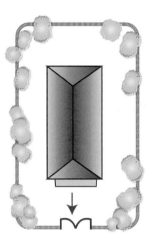

Shape C

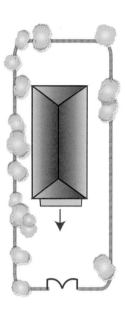

Shape B

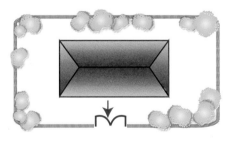

Triangular-shaped land

Triangular-shaped land is of the Fire element. It is clearly imbalanced and it is highly likely that there will be some sectors of the 8 directions that will be missing. Usually, homes built on triangular-shaped land will have sharp corners, hence, the occupants will be accident prone. The direction of the corner will dictate who will have accidents or where accidents will occur. For example, a sharp point in the East sector means leg accidents are likely to occur. It is only in the hands of a very skilful Feng Shui practitioner that triangular-shaped land can be used effectively and well, as it requires great skill when it comes to use of Water to counter the Fire element of the triangle-shaped land. Generally, it is best to avoid this type of land to save yourself hassle.

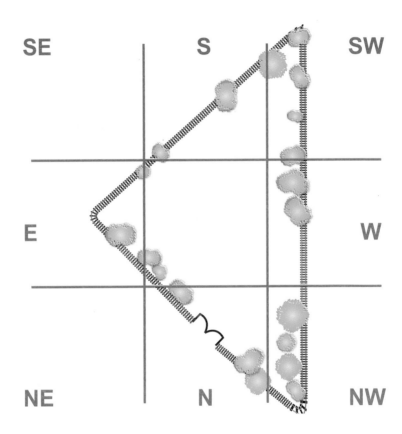

Triangular land naturally creates a sharp corner or Sha Qi

Round-shaped land

This is of course rare but I have seen cases of round/roundish-shaped land before so it is not an impossible situation. Round land focuses all the Qi into the center portion of the property. This creates very intense Qi at the central palace. Accordingly, it is generally not recommended for residential properties. Commercial properties are evaluated differently but as this is a book for Homebuyers, I will not delve into that. If however you have no choice, the house has to be positioned slightly off-center.

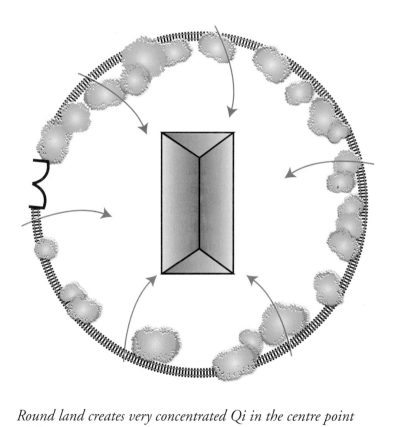

Round land creates very concentrated Qi in the centre point of the property

Oval-shaped land

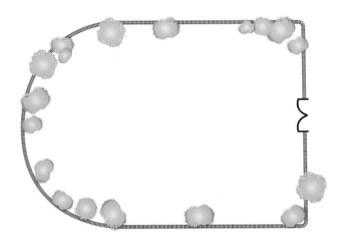

Oval-shaped land is classified as Metal element land. Generally, it is more suitable for individuals involved in Water-related businesses like travel, transport and logistics to make use of oval-shaped land. However, it is very important that your house is not located on the curved portion of the land but the square section of the land, as in the diagram below.

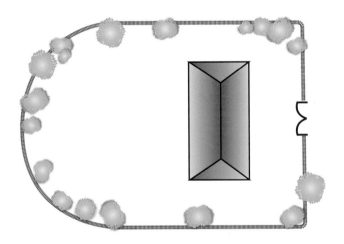

It is also important to look at the type of curve in the oval shape land. In Feng Shui, it is preferred that the curve goes outwards, so as to deflect Qi. If it curves inwards, this creates an instant Sha Qi that hits the property square on.

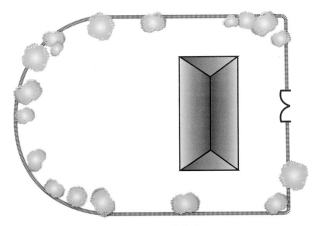

Outward curving land deflects Qi

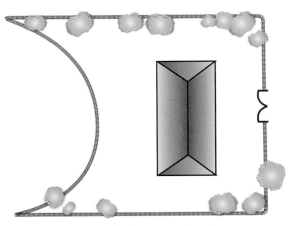

Inward curving land creates Sha Qi

Long and Oblong-shaped land

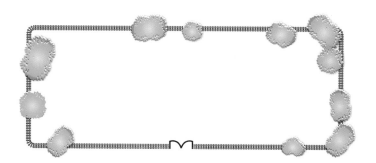

Generally, it is best to avoid buying strips of land where you have to build an elongated or disproportionate property. A house like that will have lots of alleys and it will be difficult to contain Qi or distribute it properly within the home. If you already have a piece of land like this, it is better to parcel the land into small segments or pieces and have two houses.

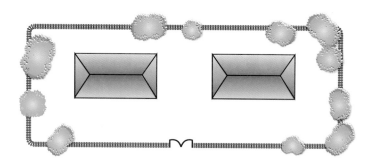

Trapezium-shaped land

There are two types of trapezium-shaped land: one type is where the front is narrow, and the back is wider; the second type has a narrow back, and a wide front.

It is preferred for trapezium-shaped land to be tight at the front and wide at the back as this makes it easier to draw in, collect and circulate Qi. Trapezium-shaped land that is wide in the front and tight at the back pushes Qi out and doesn't contain Qi well. Imagine your shirt pocket – if it is broad at the top and narrow at the bottom, your pen will keep slipping out, right?

If you have no choice but to choose land that is tight at the back and wide in front, the trick is to plant trees in the front to narrow and close off the front a little, or to cut-off the front portion into a garden, thus narrowing the front of the land.

ENVIRONMENT

Trapezium-shaped land

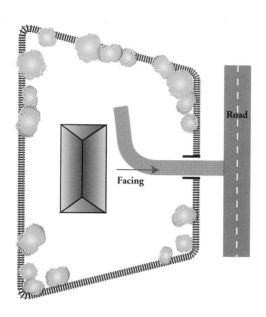

A wide back and narrow front is preferred for trapezium shaped land

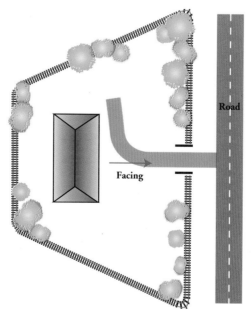

A tight back and wide front makes it hard for Qi to be contained

L-shaped land is generally not a good piece of land to select because it instantly comes with missing sectors and therefore, it very difficult to achieve balanced Qi when it comes to the 8 Guas. In addition to having built in problems, L-shaped land also comes with 'instant Sha Qi'. This type of shape creates Sha Qi because of the sharp angles in the L. This is possible to resolve by ensuring that the Main Door is not affected by the sharp edge of the land but the property will still potentially have problems with missing sectors and imbalanced Qi

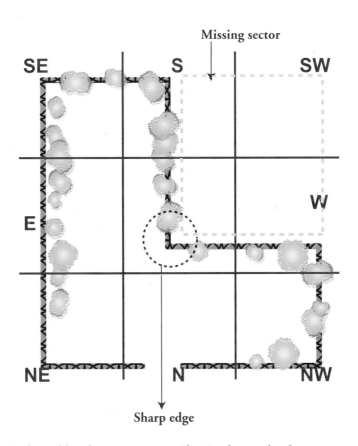

L-shaped land creates instant Sha Qi due to the sharp corner in the L

ENVIRONMENT

71

Odd-shaped land

When evaluating odd-shaped lands, the key is to look for missing sections. Generally, large pieces of odd-shaped land will be less problematic than a small piece of odd-shaped land. This is because a small piece of odd-shaped land is more likely to have missing sectors and problems with corners. If you have such a land, the answer is to get a landscape artist to help you 'square off' the land using trees and bushes.

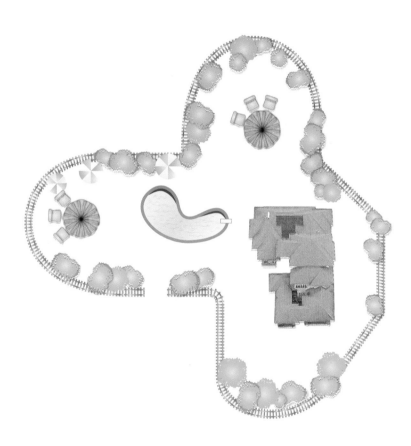

The High and Low of Land

Unless you are living in an extremely flat area, most properties will have some protrusions or raised sections. A very common question I receive from the public is whether it is okay for land to be higher at the back and does a lower front denote bad Feng Shui. Highs and lows of the land do matter and I will delve into the significance of different parts of the land being higher or lower in this section.

When selecting your land, take note of the surrounding hills and land alleviations

ENVIRONMENT

Protrusions in land

In Feng Shui, we do not make generalisations of good or bad. Rather, we are more interested in the significance of the feature. Protrusions are not necessarily good or bad – rather, it is what the impact of the protrusion is in terms of the lie of the land and where the protrusion appears. A protrusion is regarded as significant only if its mass occupies up to 1/3 of the land or its impact is to render the property into an L-shaped property.

Generally, when it comes to small protrusions, a Feng Shui consultant is usually more concerned with the sector that it impact on. So if for example, there is a protrusion in the South sector, the element of Fire is very strong in the property. If Fire is a negative element for any of the occupants of the house, then this property will be detrimental to the occupant. If however the Fire element is good for the occupants, based on certain calculations, then this protrusion is fine. As a general rule, avoid protrusions to avoid problems.

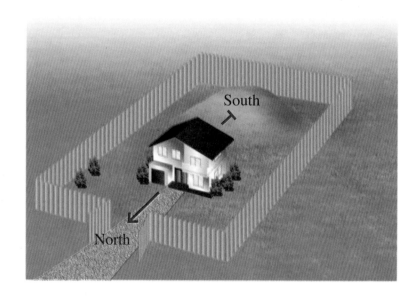

High back, low front formation

Facing

Generally, in Feng Shui practice, this is a preferred formation for property. Such a formation is preferred because the property is regarded as protected by a mountain at the rear. This formation will be even better if the back is West, Northwest, Northeast and South direction, although this must be qualified by the time factor.

Generally, we do not like the land to slope backwards at the rear of the property because the Qi then rushes out the back too quickly. This causes the internal Qi of the property to be imbalanced and the occupants will feel insecure. To help improve this situation, try to plant many tall trees at the back of the property to balance the Qi and redirect the Qi back to the property.

Trees at the back of house

Left high, right low formation

When viewed from the inside of the property, looking out, a high left side and a low right side is regarded as a good formation. In Feng Shui, this is interpreted as the Green Dragon being higher than the White Tiger and thus is considered a good formation. However, it is important to further qualify the formation, to ensure it is actually a good one. You need to make sure that the land does not slope steeply to make the property lopsided. A slight slope or incline is okay but not a substantial tilt. If the property has a substantial tilt, this will need to be corrected by planting tall trees on the right side to re-balance the Qi.

Left side

Facing

Trees at the right of house   *Left side much higher*

Facing

ENVIRONMENT

77

Right high, left low formation

Again, this is viewed from the inside of the property, looking out. When the right side is high and the left side is low, this formation is interpreted as the White Tiger being higher than the Green Dragon. This formation is generally not good for the men of the house and is generally not favourable for well-being and peace of mind of the residents. Again, we need to qualify the formation. A slight, gentle slope is not going to have a substantial impact – it is only when the right side of the property is substantially higher than the left side, that you should consider not purchasing the property.

Right side gentle slope

Facing

Right side very high

Trees at the left of house

Facing

Terraced Land

When evaluating terraced land, the issue is the depth and steepness of the terracing. If the terracing you are facing is gentle, shallow and gradual, then this is generally regarded as favourable. In advanced landform Feng Shui, this is known as "Jin Tian Shui 進田水" meaning Advancing Field Water. If the terracing is very steep, this is not good as the Qi is gushing down too fast and cannot collect. Also, fast moving and rushing Qi is considered Sha Qi (Killing Qi) and is not what we want affecting our property.

ENVIRONMENT

79

Modern concept of Advancing Field Water

When we talk about a bowl land, we are not talking about a hole in the ground with a house inside. Bowl land is not a crater in the ground. That is more like a wok-shaped piece of land and that is definitely not good because the Qi is stagnant and cannot be rejuvenated.

Bowl land

Bowl- land is more like a gentle saucer or the curvature of your palm. This is of course a very subtle distinction. A bowl land is regarded as good generally as all the Qi will converge in the land. It is an ideal location for a property. Wok-shaped land on the other hand is not good.

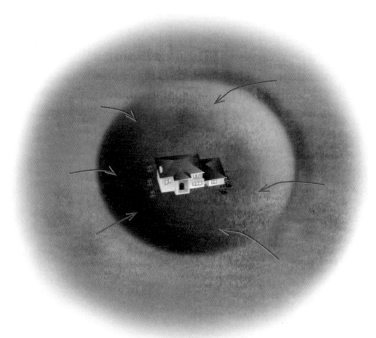

Wok-Shaped land – the Qi stagnates at the bottom.

Mound Land

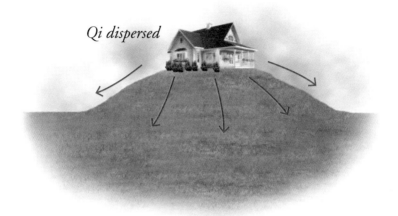

Qi dispersed

If your piece of land has contours that resemble a mound, this is generally not a good place to locate property. This is because Qi is being constantly dispersed from all corners. Qi should converge, before it is distributed. If it cannot converge in the first place, then there's no Qi entering the property.

ENVIRONMENT

83

Generally, land with a lot of large rocks and boulders is regarded as damaged land. The Qi flow and Qi itself is blocked by the stones. Now, you might be thinking: well, just remove the stones and problem solved right? Unfortunately, it's not as easy as that because rocks are, according to the classical texts, the bones of the Dragon.

Removing the bones may end up damaging the Qi of the land even more. Generally, it is best to avoid purchasing property that is on rocky land because you will need to get a Feng Shui consultant to supervise the removal of the large rocks to ensure you take out the rocks properly without damaging the land or the Qi. This is because some rocks can be safely removed while some should never be removed.

Rocky land is not conducive for Qi flow

ENVIRONMENT

We all know how this type of land feels. You know, you step on the ground and it feels like you're walking on oatmeal. Or you step on it and immediately you hear the squelch of water and mud (and it sticks to your shoes). All these indicate that the property is waterlogged. Waterlogged land is land which cannot contain Qi or allow Qi to converge or collect. In Feng Shui, soggy land is considered bad land and should be avoided. Houses built on this type of land will result in occupants with lots of illnesses or long-term poor health

The Soil of the Land

It is difficult to explain to beginners and lay persons the concept of land contours and dragon veins in a simple beginners book. But I want to give you some tools to make use of Luan Tou巒頭 Feng Shui or Classical Land Form Feng Shui. The quickest way to do this is to show you how to look at the soil of the land.

Yes, soil is important too in evaluating the quality of the land. In Luan Tou Feng Shui, different types of Mountains (Dragons) formations carry different stars and thus produce different types of soil and soil with different qualities. In Feng Shui there are nine specific stars and these nine stars refer to the stars of the North Dipper. You see, Feng Shui is a form of astrology of the land – the land is influenced by the star configurations as our planet orbits the sun. These stars subsequently form mountains through their magnetic influence on the planet. Each star has different elemental values thus the mountains that are formed by the influence of these stars are also unique and of different elemental values.

Therefore, a quick way to make use of Classical Land Form Feng Shui, without having a full and comprehensive understanding of Ru Di Yan 入地眼 or the Entering Earth Eye Classics, a central ancient text on Luan Tou Feng Shui, is to observe the soil colours. By looking at the soil colour, you can determine what mountains (dragons) are influencing the land. The trade secret of many top Feng Shui master is to check the soil to determine the quality of the land.

When it comes to checking soil, you must be careful that you are not looking at the surface soil or topsoil. This is soil that is usually placed above the original soil of the land by gardeners or by the property developer. To check the original soil of the land, you may have to dig one to two feet down in order to see the real soil.

Also, it is important to recognise that, in Feng Shui, the same stars are often used by different systems to represent different elements. A star in Eight Mansions may not have the same elemental attributes as a similarly named star in Flying Stars. When it comes to Landforms, we are studying the Qi of the land and so the elements of the Nine Stars differ. For example, a Greedy Wolf 貪狼 Mountain is wood shaped, hence it is regarded as Wood element. However in Flying Stars, Greedy Wolf is synonymous with the Star #1 and is thus Water element.

	Star	Soil Colour
1	Greedy Wolf (貪狼)	Greenish
2	Huge Door (巨門)	Slightly yellowish
3	Rewards (祿存)	Dark yellow
4	Literary Arts (文曲)	Blackish, dark coloured
5	Chastity (廉貞)	Reddish
6	Military Arts (武曲)	Pale white
7	Broken Soldier (破軍)	Metal but black-white mixture
8	Left Assistant (左輔)	Mixture of green/yellow – army camouflage colour
9	Right Assistant (右弼)	Whitish / blackish

ENVIRONMENT

Greedy Wolf   *Rewards*

Huge Door   *Literary Arts*

Now, soil colours are indeed subtle so you need to look at quite a good chunk of the soil, and not just one handful. One handful may be a mixture of topsoil and the actual soil of the land and can be deceptive in its appearance.

The different types of soil indicate the best usage of the land, in accordance with the quality of the soil. But this being a beginner's book, we'll keep it simple. Generally, try to find land with either Greedy Wolf soil, Huge Door or Military Arts soil. If you find any land with these three types of soil, this is considered superior land. The land itself will bring its occupants good fortune. The Greedy Wolf star brings reputation, honour and status, the Huge Door star brings wealth and prosperity while the Military Arts star brings power.

Rocky Soil

You may find that in addition to the colour of the soil, the qualities of the soil are important. Sometimes, you have the right colour soil but the soil is rocky – it has a lot of rocks or boulders. There are two issues to bear in mind when it comes to rocky soil. Firstly, it is expensive to utilise because you have to render the land usable in the first place by properly removing the rocks and boulders.

Secondly, land becomes rocky due to exposure to wind. When the land is cut through by strong winds, the rocks become exposed because the soil has been dispersed. Following the theory of Feng Shui, Qi is dispersed by wind and collects at the boundaries of water. Accordingly, before you consider buying land with rocky soil, you should make several visits at different points of the month to ascertain if the wind is gusting and strong. If the wind is strong, the Qi is dispersed and no property can benefit from the Qi of the environment if it is located on such a piece of land.

ENVIRONMENT

Mountains are an extremely important component when considering the environment around your property. Mountains represent bodies of Qi. The Qi in the environment is drawn from the mountains in the area. Hence, to understand what kind of Qi you can tap into in a certain area or neighbourhood, you must first observe the type and quality of mountains in the area.

Many people say they cannot see the mountains in their area but this is because their eyes are untrained. Look at the picture below of the area around the Klang Valley in Malaysia - there are mountains and hills everywhere.

Do you see the mountains?

In every country I have been to and I have travelled extensively around the world, I have seen mountains, even in areas that look flat or areas that are heavily developed. In Dallas and Toronto for instance, when I arrived at these cities, my students were adamant that their cities were 'flat'. When we started to drive around to check the Feng Shui, soon enough, they discovered that there are indeed many small hills and land contours they had not previously noticed!

So often when my students or members of the public say they cannot see hills in their area because they live in the city, it is not because there are no mountains or hills but because they simply do not perceive the mountains or hills. Look around with Feng Shui Vision and you will find they are indeed there!

Now, laypeople or beginners will probably find it difficult to judge the shapes of the mountains but you can probably discern the direction and location of the mountain (right, left, front, back). So, first, let's talk about where you would like to see mountains in proximity to your property and where you don't want to see the mountains.

Look carefully - there are high and lows in this seeming flat land

Between the years 1964 to 2043 is known as Period 6-9 in San Yuan Feng Shui. Mountains therefore should be ideally located at Northwest, West, Northeast and South sectors, measured from the center of the house using the pie method described in Chapter 2. Mountains should not be located at the East, Southwest, Southeast and North directions. Simple isn't it?

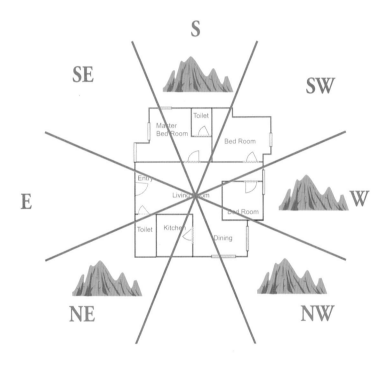

Are there exceptions to the rule? Of course. But in general, if you find mountains in the good directions listed above, you can be sure that your property is, if not superior, reasonably good, in terms of people luck till 2043. What does people luck mean? It refers to harmony in the home, good relationships between the occupants of the home and fertility.

At a higher level of study, we actually 'qualify' the type of mountain that is in the vicinity. Your classical Feng Shui practitioner, if you hire one, will inspect, study and judge the quality of these mountains in relation to your property. Their shape, movement, charisma and structure type are all key points of consideration that the Feng Shui practitioner will audit. Of course this requires much training and is beyond the scope of this book. But I mention it so that if you hire a consultant, you know what they should be looking at when they audit your property for you.

Not checking what 'type' of mountains a property is exposed to and simply addressing the internal settings (such as bed directions and door directions) is a pointless exercise as we have not ascertained the simple question of whether or not there is Qi present in the area. If you do not know what type of Qi you have in the area, how are you going to tap into the Qi?

A good Feng shui master knows what type of mountain he is looking at - This is a Chastity Star mountain

ENVIRONMENT

Mountain at the back of the property

Mountain at the back

Facing

Mountain at the back

In accordance with general Feng Shui principles, a mountain behind is seen as good support for the house. This means the Facing of the house is Yang and the back of the house or the Sitting, is Yin. Mountains in landform Feng Shui are regarded as Yin. Therefore, having a Yin feature, at the Yin location, where it SHOULD be Yin, denotes all is as it should be. All is stable and balanced. If you like, you can think of it as 'the mountain supports your house' and so there is a sense of security in the home, stability and family harmony. Not having a mountain at the back generally indicates a lack of these features. If you don't have a mountain at the back, it is not a major problem, as long as the land does not slope downwards at the back.

*Mountain behind
the house*

House facing

Mountain at the back of the property

ENVIRONMENT

Mountain in front of the property

The front or Facing of the house is Yang and the back of the house or the Sitting is Yin. When you have a mountain in front, this means the Yin feature is in front, where it should be Yang. Such a formation is regarded as generally unfavourable, in particular if the mountain is very large and/or it is too near. What is too near? Generally, if the mountain is within a radius of 30 feet of your home or property, and literally, looms up in front of you. In such instance, the property is not receiving any benefit from the mountain.

However, if the mountain is far away, then it is fine. How do you know if it is far away? Stand at the door or front of the property and stretch out your hand straight out at eyebrow level. If the top of the mountain is the same level as your hand, then the mountain is not considered a negative mountain feature. In fact, it is auspicious and desirable formation because you have what is known as a Table Mountain formation.

House facing mountains

Mountain on the left of the property

In the basic study of Landform Feng Shui or Luan Tou Feng Shui, a stretch of mountains on the left of the property (when viewed from the Main Door looking out) is considered the Green Dragon Embrace (Qing Long Sha 青龍砂). Sha here refers to embracing arms in the study of Luan Tou Feng Shui (not to be confused with the Sha Qi 煞氣). The Sha protects the property from violent Qi. The Green Dragon usually governs male prosperity in the house. If you spot a mountain on the left side of the property, be sure to check that it is not too near to the property; otherwise, instead of functioning as a protective presence, it becomes suppressive, creating a formation known as Green Dragon Suppressing the House Formation.

Mountain on the left

Facing

Mountain on the right of the property

In the basic study of forms, a stretch of mountains on the right is considered the White Tiger Embrace (Bai Hu Sha 白虎砂). Sha here refers to embracing arms in the study of Luan Tou Feng Shui. The Sha protects the property from violent Qi. The White Tiger should be at a moderate distance and not higher than the Green Dragon. If it is at the same height, then that is fine, denoting a balance of Yin and Yang. But if it is too close and very high, then the formation becomes what is known the 'White Tiger Pouncing to House Formation'. If it is close but not high, this is also not too good as it is known as ' Forcing the Tiger to Jump Over the Wall'.

Mountain on the right

Facing

*Right side is overly high
and too near to the house*

'White Tiger Pouncing to House' Formation

Observing Appearance of the Mountain

Not only do you need to identify where the mountains are in relation to your property and their direction, but their physical appearance, which forms a critical aspect in the study of Luan Tou, is of great significance. The mountains in your environment were made by nature through the millenia – man did not shape the mountains, they were shaped by the forces of nature and the magnetic pull of the stars in the universe. Therefore, their natural appearance denotes the type of Qi that is released to the immediate proximity and environment around the mountain. Hence, it is important to observe their actual appearance, to ascertain the type of Qi in the environment and the Qi the property can receive.

According to San He classics, a good Mountain is green, lush and gentle in appearance, with rounded tops. Such mountains are healthy and growing Dragons (Sheng Long 生龍) and emit benevolent Qi.

Growing Dragons 生龍

In contrast, bad mountains have steep, sharp and pointy tops, like that of a witch's hat. Mountains that have naturally collapsed are also not good – these are known as Broken Mountains. Mountains that are rocky or that have been blasted with dynamite or mined or quarried are also not good. If you see a mountain with greenery and rock together, this is not a good mountain. In the classics, this is known as a Sick Dragon (Bing Long 病龍) and denotes the Qi in the mountain does not flow well.

You have to be a bit careful if the mountains have no trees. You then have to observe all the other mountains in the range of vicinity. For example, if you have been to Las Vegas, you will notice that the mountains there are 'naked' – they have no trees. But, every single one of the mountains in Las Vegas looks the same, hence, this is acceptable. Feng Shui is not about being an individual – it is about harmony of the environment. So if all the mountains look the same, then the Qi is unified and flows well.

Sick Dragons 病龍

ENVIRONMENT

103

This may seem very easy but studying landforms is not something that can be done in a beginners book or from a book. So what I have done here is to synthesise the key information and concepts for you in an understandable and easy to apply context. I have not explained the whys here for brevity and the sake of space, but if you are interested, the best way to learn is to take a class and walk the mountains with a qualified landform expert.

Walking the Mountains is integral part of my annual, highly popular China Excursion course, where my students learn Luan Tou Feng Shui the old fashioned physical way!

FENG SHUI FOR HOMEBUYERS - EXTERIOR

Special formations are unique land structures wherein when all the criteria for the structure is fulfilled by the land, automatically the Qi in the area is regarded as superior and all that needs to be done is to receive the Qi into the house. I have included a few examples of these for those who are interested in delving a little bit deeper into Landform Feng Shui.

Green Dragon Crossing Bright Hall
Formation 青龍過堂

This formation occurs when the left embrace of the property, looking out, stretches out, then curves and crosses the front of the property. There must be a substantial distance between the front of the property and the crossing, to ensure a sufficiently large Bright Hall. By the way, a Bright Hall is a technical Feng Shui term to describe the space in front of your house. It is not a place with a lot of lights! Contrary to some popular misconceptions, you cannot create a bright hall by putting 220 megawatt lights in your porch. That is taking the concept of the 'Bright Hall' literally. Remember the Chinese are fond of highly artistic and flowery sounding names – it's just the romantic in them. They certainly didn't mean for the names to be taken literally.

Green Dragon Crossing Bright Hall

Facing

The Green Dragon Crossing Bright Hall Formation is particularly prized because it denotes a very benevolent Green Dragon – it is said in the ancient texts: the Green Dragon governs Wealth, the White Tiger governs Nobility. So when a Green Dragon crosses the property in this manner, this denotes prosperity grows and compounds with each generation. It is a rare formation but not impossible to find – I have actually myself seen several instances of this formation during my consultations in Malaysia.

Please note that you cannot MAKE this formation – it has to be natural. Often, it is a client who is going through very good Heaven Luck or one who makes a great effort to find such a formation that has the opportunity to utilise the excellent Qi from such a formation.

ENVIRONMENT

White Tiger Crossing Bright Hall Formation 白虎過堂

The counterpart of the Green Dragon Crossing the Bright hall Formation is the White Tiger Crossing Bright Hall Formation. This formation represents tremendous nobility but it carries a side-effect which is that the woman takes charge or is domineering. Now, in this day and age, this is quite acceptable, as today, most ladies have had the benefit of a good education and are often very capable in their own right. In the old days, when women had no opportunity for education or where education was the privilege of only a few ladies, the idea of a woman taking charge and leading the family was unheard of. Hence, it was considered not so desirable.

White Tiger Crossing Bright Hall

Facing

Red Phoenix Rising Formation

This formation denotes rising fame, like a phoenix. Now, this is again very symbolic language – what it means in the context of forms is that you have rising mountain behind the table mountain. It looks like the picture below. It means that the area's Qi is coagulated within the area, and is not escaping so the prosperity can last because the Qi is locked in. This type of formation can produce noble and wealthy individuals.

Red Phoenix Rising Formation

Water

Water is one of the two most important features in external environment analysis. The other is mountain. Mountain is the Yin feature of the environment, Water is the Yang counterpart. Together, Mountain and Water represent the interaction between Yin and Yang, which gives birth to Qi in the environment. So in any environment to be good, it must have a harmonious configuration of both Mountain and Water. A place with only Water and no Mountain is too Yang. A place with only Mountains and no Water is too Yin. Either alone is not desirable, balance is what we seek. Hence, it is important to observe the water in the environment in tandem with observing the Mountains.

It is not easy to observe water in the environment. Water is in itself an extensive, complex and long study that requires many years studying the ancient classics like Di Li Wu Jie 地理五訣, Shui Long Jing 水龍經, Xue Xin Fu 雪心賦 and Ru Di Yan 入地眼. But this book is designed to help you screen houses so I will show you a few easy techniques that you can use to observe water in the environment.

First and foremost, you need to be familiar with the different types and categories of water. And we're not even talking about formations! Yes, it may seem rather simple what I am asking you to observe but remember, Feng Shui is a science of observation and so, we sometimes have to be meticulous and look at both the big and small picture.

Sea Water

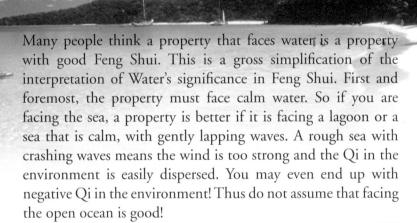

Many people think a property that faces water is a property with good Feng Shui. This is a gross simplification of the interpretation of Water's significance in Feng Shui. First and foremost, the property must face calm water. So if you are facing the sea, a property is better if it is facing a lagoon or a sea that is calm, with gently lapping waves. A rough sea with crashing waves means the wind is too strong and the Qi in the environment is easily dispersed. You may even end up with negative Qi in the environment! Thus do not assume that facing the open ocean is good!

Another key point to remember, if your property is facing the sea - ensure that you see a 'mountain' in the distance or beyond the horizon. You might be thinking – mountain in the sea, what is this? Go to Penang in Malaysia. Visit Hong Kong. You will find that these are cities which face the sea, but with islands in the distance, that serve to lock the Qi and prevent it from dispersing. It is only in this instance that having sea water in the front is desirable.

If you own a beach house, and live full time at the beach house, you need to make sure you have these features. If you do not, then just make the house a holiday home. That way, you won't be too affected by any unfavourable Qi in the area.

ENVIRONMENT

113

Lake Water/Pond Water

The waters of lakes and ponds are regarded as peaceful and sentimental water. The type of water helps collect Qi, thus if you have a lake or pond in front of your house, this is generally good. Water by itself is already Yang – in a lake form, it is known as the Yin within the Yang. Since the Qi is already sentimental, the key is to ensure that the lake is in the correct location in relation to your property.

Lake

Pond

Waterfall

This is beautiful to the eyes but gushing water, especially if the waterfall produces a thunderous sound, is considered negative Qi. Contrary to popular belief, the sound of gushing or clashing water is considered a negative feature. Qi cannot collect in such an area and you may even end up with negative Qi or Sound Sha. You don't want to create a waterfall in your property for this reason. This form of Sha Qi is damaging to career prospects as well as the mental well-being of the residents. Now of course, to generate a substantially thunderous sound, you need water to drop from 6-7 feet and for this to be a continuous affair. Accordingly, Crying Walls (a type of modern decorative wall that has water dripping from the top to bottom like a curtain) are not dangerous and showers are fine!

Drains are common in tropical climates where there is a lot of rain and external drainage and internal drainage is required. Sometimes, drains can be favourable but most of the time, they are an unfavourable feature. We are not talking about the little drains in your house that lead from your kitchen to the outside. We are talking about a deep drain where water is constantly flowing. If such a drain has a constant flow of water, cuts across your main door, within 8 or less feet, this is considered very negative Feng Shui formation called Cutting Feet Water. Cutting Feet Water is one of the most dangerous negative water formations as it blocks out all positive Qi from entering the property. It is considered one of the major Killing Qi formations and is very unfavourable for the health and wealth of the property's occupants.

It is important when such a feature is visible in a property, to cover up the drain. Obviously, if it is a monsoon drain outside your home, you cannot cover this easily. So try to conceal it out of sight – for example, place concrete slabs over the drain, especially where the drain comes close to the front of your property. If it is not possible to close off or cover the drain in the opinion of your contractor, then it is best to avoid this particular property.

Monsoon drain

ENVIRONMENT

117

FENG SHUI FOR HOMEBUYERS - EXTERIOR

You should be aware of large drains near the property

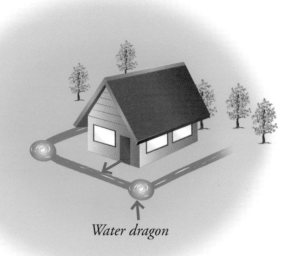

Water dragon

Many people are under the impression that creating a drain or drainage around their house, that enters the house and exits the house at certain angles, crossing the frontage of the house, is a 'Millionaire Water Dragon' formation. This is sometimes touted as a secret formula for creating immense wealth. Don't be fooled. For a water formation to be truly effective, it must be natural and part of the environment. This is not impossible, but is tedious to find, difficult to properly use and requires a genuinely qualified professional Feng Shui Master with expertise in applying the Ru Di Yan 入地眼 and Xue Xin Fu 雪心賦 classics' methodology.

Some practitioners today opt to 'make drains' in the form of a dragon in the house garden – this is a highly dangerous and problematic task as the 'structure' of these Water Dragons may end up creating Sha Qi or Killing Qi and thus cause the residents untold problems. Making your own is not only not effective

ENVIRONMENT

but can even be dangerous – you may end up with Cutting Feet Water that cuts into the Qi of the house and causes negative Qi. Creating an effective water flow needs land space and must be supported by the right mountain formations – remember the rule of Yin and Yang? Water must be balanced with Mountain in order to utilise a Water formula effectively. In Feng Shui, the forms must come first, before the formula. You cannot make what nature does not create in the environment this way so be forewarned.

So if you are taken to a house and told it has a Water Dragon built into it by the previous owner, it is best to pass or get it verified by a proper Feng Shui consultant before you decide to buy the property.

Cutting feet water

*A man-made drain supposedly representing a Water Dragon
outside a house*

If there is a manhole that is visible within a close proximity of the front of the property, there is a Qi puncture problem. This can occur even if the manhole is covered by a grill. If it is within your house compound, it is best to cover it up using an earth slab.

Flowing water denotes Qi that is circulating and indicates that the Qi renews itself and that the environment is vibrant and constantly being rejuvenated. Stagnant water denotes lifeless and stuck Qi, which does not renew and rejuvenate. Its vibrancy is limited and thus, the use of the water is also very limited since its Qi is diminished. Remember that Water is the Blood of the Dragon. If it doesn't flow, you have a blood clot problem. What you want is a moderate sentimental circulation – not too fast, not too slow.

Flowing water

Stagnant water

Naturally, we prefer clean water. Clean water denotes that
the water is vital and vibrant. Clean water denotes the Qi is
vibrant and the occupants of the property are wealthy and the
wealth Qi is vibrant. Dirty Water is equivalent to poison in
the environment – areas with dirty water usually have a lot
of problems with insects, vermin and vector illnesses. The Qi
cannot be properly harnessed when water is not clean, causing
bad health, poor performance and bad wealth luck for the
occupants in the area.

Clean water

Dirty water

The Sound of Water

When it comes to water, you need to observe not just the water, but you need to judge and hear the sound of water. Gently rippling, gurgling water denotes gentle and harmonious Qi flow, bringing about peace of mind, a relaxed environment and good performance at work. It is often said (incorrectly that is) that Water brings Wealth in Feng Shui. This is the real reason why Water brings wealth – if you live healthily, perform well, then of course, success and money arrives. If you live in an environment where water is always gushing and thunderous, the sound of water clashing and it is noisy, do you think you can excel?

Why are houses that leak badly considered bad, not just in Feng Shui but generally? It is not the leak that is problem, it is the constant dripping noise. The idea of 'water torture' is torment created by the noise of dripping water and the sensation of dripping water, drop by drop, on a person's head. Feng Shui recognises that persistent, dripping noise, is irritating and therefore disruptive to the person's health and vitality.

Why do people lose money when the house leaks? This is because the leak affects the Qi flow of the house and of course, the constant dripping of water disrupts the performance of the occupants and affects their vitality. When you are not healthy and sharp, you cannot perform. Physically, the sound is highly irritating and a nuisance and is considered Sound Sha. That is why in the old days, people didn't live near mountains because the dripping sound of water down the stalactites would be immensely disruptive.

Water can be located in a number of possible locations and directions around your property. There are different interpretations. In this section, I will show you a few possible formations and also explore some special and unique water formations.

Water at the back of the house

It is a common misconception that water at the back of the house is bad Feng Shui. This is because the back is supposed to be Yin, and the front is supposed to be Yang. Hence, when there is water at the back, Yin and Yang are out of place. If house is sitting on Yang (Water), facing the Yin (Mountain), the house is said to be disharmonious and fights over money occur since water governs the Career and Wealth aspects of the house usually.

However, if the water is in a distance and beyond the water there is a mountain and/or the water is located in a suitable location according to San Yuan Xuan Kong Direct/Indirect Spirit principle, then the property may not be bad. As a side note, the word 'spirit' here does not refer to the spooks or supernatural apparitions, it's a direct translation of the term 'Shen' which refers to the bodies of Qi in an area. But to err on the side of safety or avoid problems, it is best to avoid water at the back.

Water behind houses

If however you happen to have a property with water behind, then check against the Ba Gua Directions and attributes to know what the effect of the water is. For example, if the Water is in the South, South represents the heart. If there is water hitting the South, then there will be heart-related problems or vision related issues, which correspond to Li Gua, for the occupants. The Ba Gua attributes will be able to give you the details you need on 'what' effect the water would have on the occupants of the home.

back of houses

Water behind houses

*A river immediately behind the property is generally not good
Feng Shui.*

Water in front is considered a 'Yang feature' in the Yang location. This is ideal generally, provided it satisfies the criteria for location of water in accordance to the San Yuan Direct and Indirect Spirit principle. The San Yuan Direct and Indirect Spirit explains which sectors in the vicinity of a property is suitable for water positions in which period of time. Generally from 1964 until 2043, the East, South East, North and South West are good for water. (For details as to why this is so, you need to understand the concept of San Yuan's Qi cycle).

Water on the left

Water flowing or located on the left of the property, when looking out, is called the Green Dragon Swimming in Water Formation. This is because the left side of the property is regarded as the Green Dragon. This is considered a desirable formation for wealth and prosperity of the house generally. Of course the actual Feng Shui quality of this situation is dependant on two additional qualifiers: first, it must fit the San Yuan Direct/Indirect Spirit principle and secondly, it must satisfy the Flying Star chart and/or the Xuan Kong Da Gua assessment of the property.

Water on the left

Facing

There is a myth out there that says Water on the left increases wealth and water on the right results in the husband having an affair! I want you to know that this is not true and in fact, is a misconception of an old housewives superstition. Like many things in Feng Shui, it has grown a life of its own and instead of being a qualifying principle, has become an all-encompassing unqualified rule.

In fact, the presence of water on the right side of the property, when looking out, is a formation known as White Tiger Drinking Water and can, if used correctly, be a good formation and mean that the occupants of the home have the ability to wield great power. Water on the right does not necessarily only relate to husbands and extra-marital affairs. It has other significance as well! One should always confirm the water formation with the proper assessment of the formulas before coming to a conclusion. If the water location conforms to the San Yuan Direct / Indirect Spirit principle or a specific Xuan Kong Da Gua principle, this water may bring about great benefits in terms of authority, status and recognition.

water on the right

Facing

ENVIRONMENT

133

Water above the house

Many people think that water above the house is a bad formation because in the Yi Jing (sometimes called the I Ching) there is a trigram that says water above the head denotes suffocation inside water or drowning. This has been taken to extremes, to the extent that a house with a blue roof is now regarded as a case of water above the house.

This is, as my British students like to say, a total codswallop and many a blue roof house has been unfairly labelled 'bad'. This concept is just not true. You can buy a house with a blue roof, it is fine. Water above, such as having a water tank in the roof, is fine. Even a roof swimming pool, such as is commonly found in high-end apartment buildings these days, is also perfectly fine. Remember, when it comes to water in Feng Shui, it is all about where it is located and whether or not you are affected personally by this water location. If the location of the water doesn't affect any of the occupants in your home, then it is not a problem to you!

Water above the house

Just as there are various special mountain formations, there are also various water formations that denote a good circulation of Qi in the environment where the property is located. The reason why we want to see Water is because Water is the carrier of Qi and what circulates the Qi in the area. A good water formation pulls in the positive Qi and siphons out the negative Qi. Hence, the importance of looking for good water formations. It is for this reason that you want to avoid areas with negative water formations – the Qi that comes in is already negative. Why invest in a property which needs to be fixed before it can be improved?

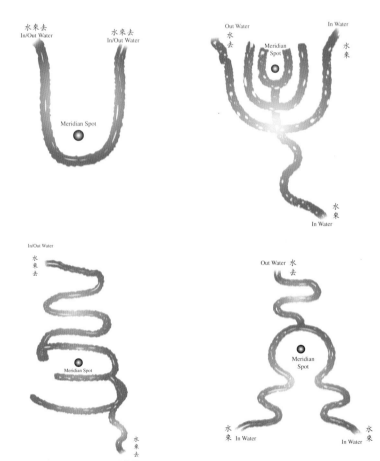

Jade Belt Formation 玉帶水

Jade Belt Water is where water curves around the property and circulates around the property, it is known as Jade Belt Water. Below is a birds-eye perspective visual of Mid Valley Megamall, a well-known mall in Malaysia, which I have taken from a helicopter.

Jade Belt Water

A Jade Belt Formation must be faced – you don't wear a belt with the buckle facing the back. To make use of a Jade Belt, you must face it. Only then does the Jade Belt direct the Qi to your property. This water formation is highly prized because it serves as both protective water and directional water; therefore, highly favourable to have this feature in proximity to your property.

Jade Belt Water around Mid Valley City, Kuala Lumpur

ENVIRONMENT

Bow Formation 反弓水

This is the counterpoint to the Jade Belt Formation. In this case, the Qi is directed straight at the property and also cuts into the property, causing damage to the Qi. This is regarded as a negative form of Water flow in Feng Shui and you should avoid any property that has this kind of water formation. What kind of problems will you have? Depending on what sector it cuts into, you will be able to determine the problem. For example, if the water cuts into Zhen Gua sector, Zhen Gua represents the elder son and the feet. Hence, the occupants of the home may experience problems with their feet or problems such as bankruptcy will affect the eldest son.

Bow Formation 反弓水

Nine Curve Water 九曲水

This is when the water curves and meanders, producing Nine Curves. This formation is highly prized because the water is sentimental and circulating. Secret of the trade: Nine Curve Water can also be seen in terms of roads. So if there are nine curves in the road that leads up to your home, then you have Nine Curve Water Formation. This is an extremely benevolent formation where Qi is very sentimental to the property – it denotes Wealth Qi that compounds and collects over the years, in a very smooth manner. If you live in Malaysia, pay a visit to Bukit Tunku or the Taman Seputeh area, and you will see this formation.

Some people think that Nine Curve Water can be made through having a long driveway, that has nine curves. This doesn't 'count' because the space within a property is insufficient to make such a formation and it has to be outside your property, such as roads leading into your estate and then leading to your specific property, to be truly effective.

Natural Nine Curve Water

If your house is very close to the mountain behind or built on a mountain and beside the mountain there is water flowing down periodically, such as during storms, this is known as Piercing Shoulder Water. The occupants of the home will experience constant illness due to the weakness in the supporting Mountain. Fertility problems are also likely, as well as lack of support at work or in the career of the individuals in the home – occupants in such a property will usually reach the top, and then get cut down.

Four Water converging into One Formation

This is a highly benevolent water formation and occurs where three or four sources of water converge and become one. It denotes multiple sources of income and highly benevolent Qi gathering on your property. It is usually rare but not impossible to find. A junction or cross-road does not constitute a convergence of water – that is considered water cutting across each other.

Four water converging into One Formation

By this point, you would have noticed that I make references to 'sentimental' and 'merciless' structures and formation. This is not something that is very easy to grasp but most people can usually perceive when something is 'aggressive' (merciless) and when it is 'gentle' (sentimental).

Merciless Water is where Water gushes out of the property very quickly. Generally, water that goes away from you, and which does not cross to the front of your property, is considered Merciless. For example, a sloping road in front of your house that causes water to run down very quickly when it rains, away from your home, is regarded as Merciless Water.

Merciless Water is water that gushes very quickly

Merciless Water is water that gushes away very quickly

Fast moving water next to the property is considered Sha-Qi

This is the opposite of Merciless Water. Sentimental water is water that embraces your property – for example, it crosses the front of your property. It should not cross directly in front of your house or cross in a straight line. In Luan Tou or Landforms, gently curving meandering water is considered to be more benevolent and gentle, and Qi that flows smoothly. It ushers rather than forces Qi into the property, bringing about good health and good financial prospects for the occupants.

Sentimental Water 有情水

Cascading Water 進田水

This is water that comes from a slightly high level, like a gently sloping terraced contour, towards the house. Cascading Water brings Qi into the house and depending on which sector it flows into, denotes great prosperity and fortune, as well as multiple generations of prosperity. Once again, this formation of cascading water cannot be made, it has to be natural contour that exists and is naturally formed in the environment.

Cascading water in the form of a foot path

Cascading Water 進田水

149

Roads are known as virtual water. It is quite hard for a lay person to recognise real water, but a proper Feng Shui master should be able to perceive it. However, roads are something which most people can recognise on a map. If you have a GPS system, it is even easier to check the roads that lead to your home. Roads, being virtual water, also carry Qi, and help bring the Qi towards and away from the property. In this section, I have selected a few common examples of virtual water that most people will encounter in a suburban environment.

The dreaded T-junction does not need much introduction. Everyone, even non-believers, knows that facing a T-junction is bad Feng Shui. Or is it? Yes, it is bad if the traffic that travels up and down the T-junction is intense. But if the traffic is light, then it is not a problem. The key to finding out if a T-junction is detrimental or not is to see whether it hits your Main Door or not. If it does not, it may not even be harmful, especially if traffic is low. If it does, fencing or walls or strategically planted trees can be used as trees can help dissipate some of the forceful Qi from the T-junction. Moving your door can also help resolve the problem but please note that this problem is not rectifiable using a Ba Gua mirror! That is a myth!

Facing T-junction

Curved 'Knife' Road

If a road curves inwards, towards your property, this is known as a Knife Formation. This Qi hits the property from all sides and usually leads to a lot of accidents and mishaps for the occupants. It is essential that you ensure the door does not face the curve if you have no choice but to select this property. Otherwise, it is best to avoid this property. However, if you are inside the curve, then you do not have a Knife Formation problem.

Road cutting into a house

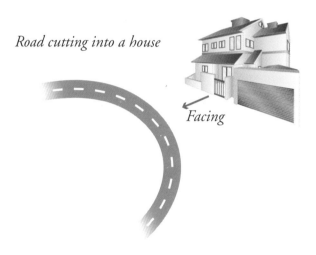

Facing

House inside the curve does not have a Knife Formation problem

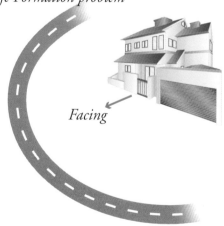

Facing

Curved 'Knife' Road

Highways are found in many developed cities these days and are a common feature in most countries. Many people are highly concerned about buying property, especially apartments which are close to highways. As a general rule, you do not want to purchase a unit of apartment or condominium that is at the same level as the elevated highway. Here's the trade secret: if you are on a level that is higher than the highway, then you are not affected by the Sha caused by the highway. In fact, if you are higher up and the highway curves sentimentally towards your unit, then you may even have a favourable situation, especially if this highway curve supports the Flying Stars of the property. As a general rule, buying the penthouse unit is probably quite safe!

House

What if your property is below the elevated highway? The key is to ensure that the shadow of the highway does not fall on your house – this is known as Yin Sha and denotes fast moving Yin Qi striking the house and diminishing the Qi. Outcomes for such homes are generally not good, wealth wise and people luck wise.

The sound from a highway can also be unfavourable. Generally properties close to highways that have sound barriers are better but try not to stay too close. If there is no sound barrier, the rushing sound of the cars is a form of Sound Sha.

ENVIRONMENT

155

FENG SHUI FOR HOMEBUYERS - EXTERIOR

House next to flyover

156

This is unstable and merciless Qi, especially if the road is very straight. Slow moving traffic is considered sentimental Qi and is more desirable. However, if you have a negative feature opposite of the road, pointing at you, then you want a fast moving road so that it blocks the negative Qi. For example, in front of the property is a graveyard but there is a road with fast moving traffic between the graveyard and your property – in this case, the road is actually a favourable feature.

If the traffic is intense and noisy, you have a problem of Sound Sha. Sleepless nights and restlessness at night anyway are simply not good for a person's health. In the case of road traffic noise, it's not just bad Feng Shui. Common sense will tell you it's a bad idea to buy property that has this problem.

Is having a house on a dead end road bad? If your property is located at the top of the dead end road or cul-de-sac, usually it is not desirable as the Qi from the road crashes straight into the house. However, properties surrounding the cul-de-sac are fine because the Qi can collect in the area in front of the house. However, if there is water in front of the house in the cul-de-sac, then all the properties, including the one at the top of the road, will benefit as the Sha Qi is blocked off by the water.

The houses surrounding the cul-de-sac are less affected, compared to the house right at the end of the road

Roundabout

A roundabout is not dangerous. In fact, it may be desirable if it is right in front of you and is a roundabout where there are many roads converging into it. This creates a virtual water formation that is similar to the four roads converging into one formation. Generally, a large roundabout is better than a small one as small roundabouts have tight curvature and so the Qi cannot circulate or collect.

If there is a small roundabout at the center of the crossroads, then it is not a problem. But if the crossroad has no roundabout in the center, make sure the traffic is not frequent and light. As long as traffic is light, the Qi flow is considered to be positive. Slightly active Qi is okay and with the right placement of the main door of your house, the Qi can be effectively tapped. If you have a house at a crossroad that looks like a cross, then you must make sure the door does not face any of the sharp points from the crossroad. Finally, make sure the crossroad junction is located in a suitable area according to the Xuan Kong Flying Star chart.

Sloping Up Road

This feature usually means that your house is located up a hill. The steepness of the road is the main criteria. Make sure the gradient is not too steep or the Qi will slip and escape. If it is, foothills in front will help trap the Qi. Generally, property at the top of the road is more suited for people in politics or those holding high public positions.

An example of upward sloping road

Sloping Up Road

Sloping Down Road

If your house is located at the bottom of a hill for example, the main thing to observe is the gradient of the road. When the slope comes towards your house gently, this is good for business. However, if the road is higher than your house and plunges steeply towards your house, it becomes Sha Qi and transforms into an aggressive form of Qi that hits your property.

An example of downward sloping road

Alleys between properties that face or point at the property cause sharp Qi to hit your property square on. This is most unfavourable and you should avoid selecting such a property. If you must buy such a property, plant trees to block the Qi and most importantly, ensure the Main Door does not face the alley square on.

Houses should not face an alley

Open spaces

In some places and cities, there are no lakes or ponds but there is an open space. It is here that Qi collects. These open spaces are in effect virtual ponds and lakes. There are many examples of such places – think Times Square and Madison Garden in New York, Trafalgar Square, Hyde Park, Taman Jaya in Petaling Jaya, Malaysia. Or it could just be a field or playground in the area.

Generally properties or houses near these areas benefit from Qi that collects there but there are some qualifiers. However, generally, if the open space is visible from the property, it is usually good. If the roads exit the park and curve towards your house in a gentle, sloping or curving manner, this is even better.

FENG SHUI FOR HOMEBUYERS - EXTERIOR

Qi collects in open spaces in the city

Golf Course

This brings some instant advantages to owners who are golfers but may not necessarily be good Feng Shui. Although golf courses qualify as open areas, it is important to study the contours of the land and also, to see where the ponds are as the location of water may negatively affect surrounding properties.

Playgrounds

Although by and large favourable as they represent open spaces where Qi can collect, there can be some negative features. See-saws pointing at your house for example are a negative feature. The corner of the field can also be a sharp corner or negative feature, especially if it points at your house. In the Flying Star Classical text, Shen Shi Xuan Kong Xue 沈氏玄空學, Principle No 30 says the corner of fields is a negative Qi and when the #5 Yellow star arrives, it denotes accidents and health issues for the occupants of a property with a field corner problem.

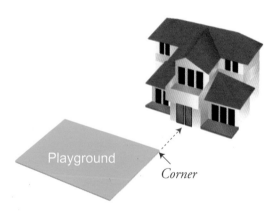

Playground

Corner

The corner of a field facilitates negative Qi

Chapter Four:
The Internal Environment

In chapter 3, I covered the key aspects of evaluating the external environment surrounding your property. In this chapter, we move to the immediate environment of the property, which I will refer to as the 'Internal Environment'.

I cannot emphasise this point enough: the external environment must support the internal environment. In Feng Shui, you can't improve the external using the internal substantially. Building a rock mountain in your garden will not in any way, compensate for the absence of a real mountain in the vicinity. But if you already have a good external environment (the right mountains, water in the right place), then your internal environment is used for fine-tuning the Qi in the environment and to tap the Qi precisely, for maximum benefit to the occupants.

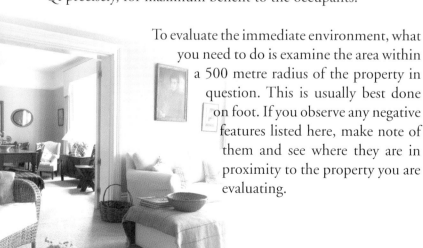

To evaluate the immediate environment, what you need to do is examine the area within a 500 metre radius of the property in question. This is usually best done on foot. If you observe any negative features listed here, make note of them and see where they are in proximity to the property you are evaluating.

Some very important advice: do not be paranoid if you do see any negative features – remember, negative features do not give rise for concern if they do not actually affect your property (for example, you find a sharp roof corner but it doesn't point at your property or your Main Door) or it does not affect the occupants in your home specifically. First observe, then analyse before you come to a conclusion.

Many people look at the building first and check all the internal Feng Shui (where the rooms are, beams in the rooms, mirror opposite front door) but forget about looking at the immediate environment and the macro, larger scale environment. Always remember this mantra: check the external environment, before you check the building.

Like land, buildings are also Qi containers. The building enables you to collect and harness the Qi in the environment, or reduce and prevent the impact of negative Qi. But what Qi you harness and whether or not you can harness and tap into the Qi using the building is entirely dependant on what is in the environment surrounding the building.

Now, when it comes to analysing buildings, formula-based calculations to assess the Qi flow and to know the Qi map of the building are usually required, utilising either Flying Stars, Eight Mansions, San Yuan, San He or Xuan Kong Da Gua. However, as this is a beginner's book for laypersons to use, I will not delve into that. But I have included in this book some diagrams and photographs that should help you evaluate buildings to a degree, with regard to their efficacy and usefulness as Qi containers.

For those of you who have some knowledge or understanding of Eight Mansions or Flying Stars Feng Shui, the main thing to remember is that even if you find negative Qi in certain sectors of the building, the negative Qi may not be activated if the building is structured in a manner that neutralises or ensures the negative Qi is not stimulated. In Feng Shui, there is a principle which states: "Forms activate the stars, stars in turn, affect the residents". Forms here means Landform. But did you know that the building's structure can also be regarded as a form that influences the stars?

What does this mean? In essence, positive forms or positive building structure can negate the impact of negative stars simply because the structure of the building does not activate or prevents the activations of negative stars.

Here's an example. Let's say, after plotting the Flying Star chart of the property, you determined that you have a 5-2 negative star combination sector in the house.

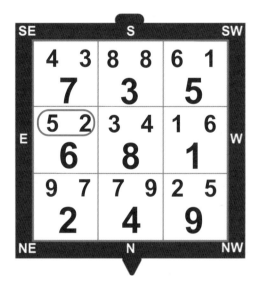

Now, in Flying Stars Feng Shui, a "5 and 2" star combination is considered a highly negative combination and so the sector in which this combination appears is considered unfavourable. Many people are accordingly fearful of sleeping in this sector as it denotes bankruptcy or bad health. This is a misconception. Here is the truth: For the 5-2 star combination to actually exert its negative effects, it has to be activated by two factors: external negative factors outside the sector itself such as pylons, a T-junction or sharp mountains or it is activated by negative structures within the sector, such as overhead beams or if the room in question is a triangular shaped room.

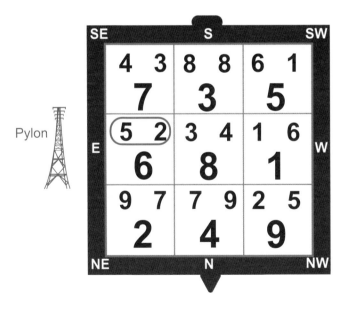

People also sometimes forget the importance of the time factor. It is usually when the annual #5 Yellow star resides in that particular sector that the 5-2 star combination will become activated and exerts its negative effects. If the house has positive features externally at the sector and positive features internally in the 5-2 sector, then the 5-2 is not negative. This of course comes at a price: the positive features that suppress and neutralise the 5-2 combination's negative effects will not exert their positive effects. So the end result is a zero sum gain.

My main suggestion for those of you who have some familiarity with formula-based calculations is not to be too fearful. If you think about it and use what I like to call 'the secret art of common sense' you will realise that every Flying Star chart and every Eight Mansions direction has both good and bad sectors!

The point is this: you don't need to fix everything. Sometimes the house and the environment will take care of it for you at no cost. The idea of Feng Shui is to use it to help you, not make it scare you into undertaking massive renovations or buying trinkets and figurines to neutralise the Qi. The best cure is no cure!

Note where the pylons are located

Let's assume you have done your homework and already checked the macro environment of the area by driving around the area. You have determined the position and location of the various mountains or hills in the area. You have also marked out where the water (both real and virtual water) is located. You have determined that the macro environment of the property you have in mind is fairly good.

Now, you can turn your attention to the building itself. The built-up area of the property is the first consideration for internal evaluation but we also need to look at the appearance and shape of the building. Remember that suitability of the facades, shape of roof and houses varies from person to person and is largely dependant on your personal element.

There is no such thing as good or bad but a question of suitable or not suitable and whether or not the occupant can make use of the structure or not. But for the purposes of screening, I have given some broad perimeters of what types of structures are generally suitable for what kind of businesses or occupants. For a more precise evaluation, a professional Feng Shui consultant's opinion should always be sought.

This is normally the frontage of the building, sometimes called the Facing of the building in Feng Shui terminology. The first thing you should check is to see if the façade is balanced or tilted.

Façade

The facing of the building should not be lopsided (meaning, leaning right or left), tilted forward or slanting backwards. The facing of a building should be like a person standing upright - it should be straight. Only then, the Qi that enters the property is sentimental, stable and every resident can live harmoniously in the building.

Examples of tilted facades on houses

Tilted facade

Roof Shape

Now, usually when we meet a person, after the face, the thing most of us tend to notice is hair! It's the same with buildings. After you have checked the façade of the building, look at the roof.

The roof should be balanced. A definite no-no is any property with a roof that slopes inwards at the center. Now, obviously, for aesthetic or unique design purposes, some properties are built with inward sloping roofs. In Feng Shui, we prefer for the center of the roof to be flat or if possible, slightly higher. A flat or slightly higher center point in the roof denotes balanced Qi. By contrast, a roof with a center that slopes inwards exerts pressure on the central palace of the property, known as the Heavenly Heart. A roof that slopes inwards is like a knife piercing the heart of the property.

Roof sloping inwards at the center, pressuring the Central Palace.

By having a roof that is slightly raised in the centre, you are protecting the center of the home, and ensuring the Qi at the center of the property is stable and protected.

THE INTERNAL ENVIRONMENT

Sharp triangular roofs are regarded as fire-shaped roofs and denotes that Fire Qi is very strong in the property. Usually if Fire Qi is very strong in the property, the house is not peaceful as Fire is volatile in nature. However, if Fire is a favourable element to the occupants of the home, then a triangular roof is fine. Generally, sharp roofs are better for spiritual places such as temples and churches, and not so suitable for homes.

Usually, most roofs are triangular. Hence, only really steep, sharp roofs are considered strong Fire element.

Flat roofs are regarded as Earth element. Therefore, these are best for educational institutions, businesses and homes as it denotes stability.

Dome roofs are considered to be Metal element. Therefore, these are best for military establishments, military bases or space observatories.

Metal shape building

Lopsided roof

A lopsided roof denotes an imbalance in the Qi – when Yin and Yang are imbalanced, growth is abnormal, emotions are unstable and people are indecisive. Accordingly, it is best to avoid a property with a lopsided roof.

Irregular-shaped roofs or roofs with no particular shape are regarded as being of the element of Water. These are best suited for academic institutions or for occupants who are writers. It is also generally good for occupants in the trading or logistics businesses.

Protruding Roofs

These are roofs where one particular part of the roof protrudes outwards, like a tree springing forth from the ground. Protruding Roofs are naturally regarded as Wood-shaped. Such roofs are good for businesses that involve development and growth, perseverance and drive, and are good for occupants who are teachers, preachers or property developers.

Protruding roof

Building Design

The overall design of the building does play an important role because it is the container of the Qi. Hence, the shape of the building plays an important part in the ability of the building to harness the Qi in the environment.

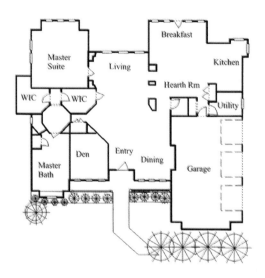

Buildings with pyramid shapes denote strong Fire Qi and are usually better for spiritual purposes. It is only suitable for occupants who can use Fire Qi or for certain businesses and this is only if the internal usage of the Water element is correct and the interior layout is correctly aligned.

U-shaped houses

The extent of the U curvature is the key qualifier when it comes to determining the suitability of a U-shaped house. A U-shaped house is generally not good if it is very small as this indicates a missing sector. However if it is a large house with many rooms, it is acceptable because the U shape becomes like the equivalent of a left and right embrace. All that needs to then be done is to internally divide the property into three wings using internal doors, thus ensuring the Qi is intact and in balance. If the house is U shaped with no internal demarcation, then you have a missing body of Qi in the house and this could lead to calamitous situations.

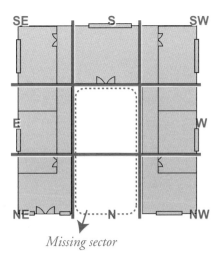

Missing sector

The center of the house ends up being outside the house when it comes to L-shaped houses. As mentioned earlier, the center of the property, the Heavenly Heart is extremely important. It is known as the central tai qi and is the core of the house's Qi. Once the central tai qi has been shifted to outside the house, it is no longer protected and the Feng Shui of the home instantly is unfavourable. The residents will feel extremely agitated and unhappy. The way to fix this situation is to demarcate the house into sections A and B (see next page), thus making the house square.

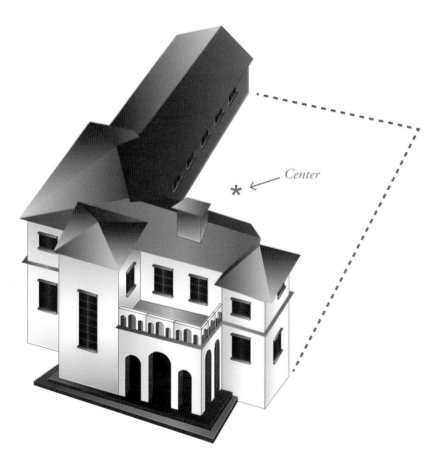

Center

*

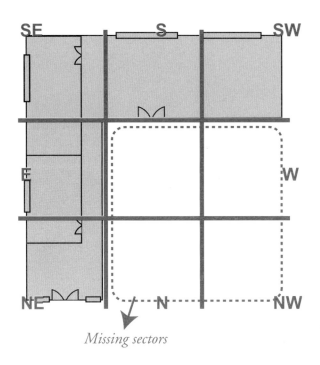

Missing sectors

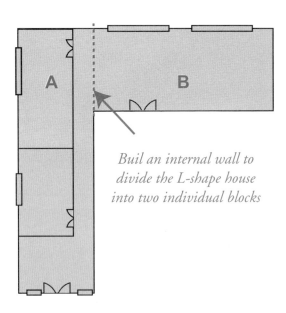

*Buil an internal wall to
divide the L-shape house
into two individual blocks*

This is the best shape generally for property. Some chipped off sectors are okay because as long as the missing sector does not constitute more than one-third of the property, then it is not considered actually missing. Now, you might be wondering: how do I know if more than one third of the sector is missing? It's simple: just divide up the property into three sections, as in the diagram. If more than 1/3 of any of the sections is missing, then you have a serious missing sector problem.

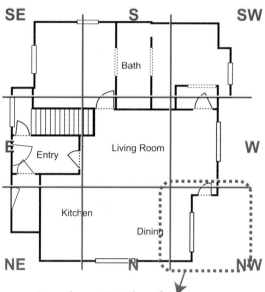

Less than 1/3. Therefore not considered missing sector

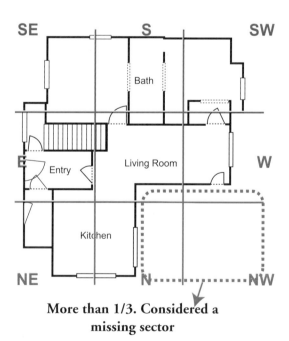

More than 1/3. Considered a missing sector

Fences, Gate and Driveways

These are the sentinels and protectors of your home. Fences help to direct, coagulate or re-direct Qi. For example, T-junction roads, negative poles or sharp corners from your neighbour can be resolved through fences. However, incorrectly placed or constructed fences can be problematic.

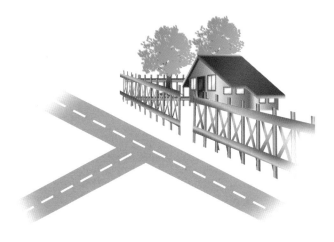

Fence that points inwards

These are sometimes used to deter or prevent trespassers but it is important to make sure that the tips of the fence do not point at your house or your neighbours house. Ideally, they should point upwards. However, these types of fences also denote very aggressive and strong Fire Qi so unless your personal element requires or can make use of Fire Qi, it is best not to have these kinds of fences at all.

Fence points inwards

Gaps in the fence are usually deliberately placed there for aesthetic purposes. Cracks however are usually more common due to damage or an actual crack that has occurred over the years. In landform, a gap or a crack is known as a wind-gap and it causes your home to be hit by wind in an aggressive manner. Generally, this is not good but again, it depends on which sector it hits and whether or not it actually affects any of the occupants in the home.

It is not good to have a fence that is the same height as your house. Yes, this ensures privacy from peeping neighbours but it also means the Qi in that sector is suppressed. When Qi is stagnant, there is a lack of growth and development amongst the occupants of the home.

House hidden inside

FENG SHUI FOR HOMEBUYERS - EXTERIOR

House is hidden inside

Try not to choose a property where the fence is very tight to the side of the house. This denotes trapped Qi and Qi that cannot circulate. The occupants of the home will experience a lack of growth or an absence or lack of advancement in life.

Fence close to the house

Gates to your Home

The gate to your home is the Qi Mouth to the property. It should always be located in a sector that is conducive towards Qi flow. The direction of the gate opening is not important (we are not concerned with whether it opens in or out) but where it is in the context of the piece of land is very important.

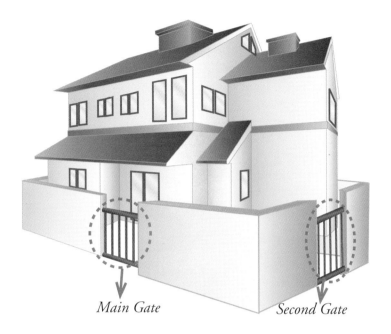

Main Gate   *Second Gate*

There should always be only ONE main gate to the house. If a property has two equal sized gates, then there are two Qi mouths and there is an influx of Qi into the property. As a result, the Qi is confused. To resolve this problem, make sure the second gate is smaller.

Two gates in the house also denotes what the Chinese call 分家 (Fen Jia). This means literally to divide up the property of the family and denotes a family splitting apart or members of the family going their separate ways, each holding onto a piece of the family crown jewels as it were. This is because the Qi of the property is divided into two. If you have a large piece of land and you know exactly which sector to place your second gate, than two gates is permissible. If not, in the event you intend to buy two terrace houses or link houses together, close up one of the gates or close both the gates and open up the gate in the middle of the property.

THE INTERNAL ENVIRONMENT

Curve of the driveway

A curving driveway gives a home a certain grandeur but you should make sure that your driveway curves the correct way. In Feng Shui, a driveway that curves inwards, towards the home, is a blade cutting into your house and a form of internal Sha Qi. If water is not positioned at the right place to slow down the Qi, then Sha Qi will hit the home.

The curved driveway in this house creates Blade Sha

Some properties are heavily shadowed as a result of high or tall trees growing in front or on either side of the property. A small amount of shade is okay but a substantial shadow is not good because this means the Qi flow to the house is blocked. The problem is easy enough to solve: just get your gardener to trim the trees or thin the trees to let in a little more light and enable the Qi to come through.

If the trees cast a shadow over your main door, this is considered a negative feature, known as Yin Sha. Yin Qi penetrates the house in such a formation. In the old days, homes with this type of negative feature were considered ghost houses or house where occupants see apparitions. In fact, the reason is that because of the Yin Sha, the mental health of the occupants is disturbed.

Trees that practically cover the Main Door

Too many trees at the gate and fence area

FENG SHUI FOR HOMEBUYERS - EXTERIOR

Where Sunlight doesn't reach the Main Door

If buildings in front of your home are very high or the fence next to your home is too high, and your home or main door is always in a shadow, this is not good because the property becomes too Yin. Growth and health or career advancement for the occupants in the home is a major problem.

Main door

No sunlight reaches this main door

Of course, the neighbourhood that you are going to reside in matters and what I mean here by your neighbours is not literally the people who live next door to you, but what is next door to you, or in close proximity to your property. Just like noisy real-life neighbours can be a real pain, so having a negative 'neighbour' can also give rise to a negative impact on your property.

Many people are afraid of living near or next to a graveyard. Obviously, burial areas are Yin areas and it is not good to have an overly Yin place near your home. However, these days, most graveyards and cemeteries are clean and beautiful and therefore, do not necessarily embody negative Qi. If anything, living near a graveyard has a psychological rather than Feng Shui effect.

If there is a road between the house and the graveyard, and the road is busy and active, then any Yin Qi from the graveyard will be dispersed by the busy road. Hauntings or ghosts in such areas are most likely the work of an overactive imagination.

Houses   *Graveyard*

The houses on the Left side of this image are not affected by the graveyard located on the right because of the busy road that segregates the two areas

Schools are considered Yang Qi. A school is usually always busy and noisy, and therefore it is considered a Yang area. Many people think the more Yang Qi they have near the home, the better. Remember, you don't want too much Yang or too much Yin – balance, that is the bottom line of Feng Shui. Living next door to a school is usually not detrimental or negative in Feng Shui but common sense will tell you it may be disruptive to sleep, which may not be that good for the health of the occupants.

Temple

Temples are spiritual grounds and are considered Fire Qi. There is a saying in Chinese – temples in all four directions, produce widows. Is this true? Why does it produce widows? Here's the explanation: spiritual grounds are not places for attraction between the sexes. People who are spiritual practitioners are usually hermits who are not interested in relationships, except their relationship with the higher powers of the universe. Therefore it is associated with being sacred and celibate. Hence, the saying that temples in four directions produce widows. It doesn't really mean women who's husbands have passed on. Rather, it means people (men and women) who have lonely and solitary lives.

Of course, there are exception to these general principle. Since temples are Fire Qi, the appropriate use of the Water element and/or Qi mouth (your door or main gate) can easily resolve this matter. And, if Fire Qi is good for the property, then this may even be beneficial.

Petrol station/Gas Station

Petrol/Gas stations are considered to be Fire element. The main thing to consider when you have a petrol/gas station as your neighbour is whether or not the Fire element is beneficial to your property, according to Xuan Kong or other Feng Shui calculations.

In general, basic Feng Shui dictates that living too close to an overly strong Fire element denotes loneliness and lack of progress. Again, the solution is the appropriate positioning of water within the house's compound.

Power substations are regarded as Fire element structures. Now, it is a myth that Fire burns away all wealth. If Fire is beneficial to your property according to Xuan Kong Flying Stars or Xuan Kong Da Gua calculation or beneficial to your personal element, then there's nothing wrong with living next to a power substation. We are more concerned with exposed electric pylons than we are with substations in Feng Shui. Of course, the electromagnetic fields from the substations may well be a cause for concern health-wise but substations in themselves have no substantial Feng Shui impact.

This is piercing merciless Qi, much like the piercing merciless Qi of a highway. The main thing to consider is which sector it pierces and also, whether or not the station casts a shadow on your house, thereby blocking the Qi from entering your home. Generally, try to avoid property close to the LRT line or station.

Pedestrian Bridge

This is a negative feature, when it is very close to your property. It is piercing Qi that hits the house or property and should be avoided generally. Of course, if it is far from your property, then there's nothing to worry about.

Pedestrian Bridges

What's Bothering You

In this section, I will talk about some of the common types of environmental features that could be of significance to the Qi flow of your property. The reason why these features 'bother you' is because they either obstruct the flow of Qi to your property or emanate negative Qi by virtue of their shape or placement, towards your property. This is not an exhaustive list but a collection of some of the more common and typical environmental features that can be found in urban neighbourhoods around the world.

Little fire hydrants look innocuous but if it is in front of the Main Door of your shoplot, this is a problem. As it cannot be removed, it is best not to chose a shoplot where the opening is obstructed by a hydrant. If you find a house you like and there is a hydrant, as long as it is not smack in front of the Main Door, it is fine.

Pylons

This is one of the most dangerous environmental features. In Feng Shui, pylons are regarded as a sharp negative object. Pylons exert an extremely negative impact if it is located directly in front of the Main Door. A Pylon located within a 100 feet radius of the property is usually a problem. A Feng Shui consultant will be able to ascertain the impact based on the corresponding animal sign year or in the corresponding Gua of that sector. So let's say in a certain property, the pylon is located in the Northwest 1 sector, Dog (Xu 戌) direction as measured from the Main Door of the house. In the year of the Dog (Xu 戌), where the Grand Duke (Tai Sui 太歲) is in the Dog (Xu 戌) direction, that will be the year when the house occupants will experience difficulties, especially related to the head because Dog (Xu 戌) is Qian Gua and represents the brain.

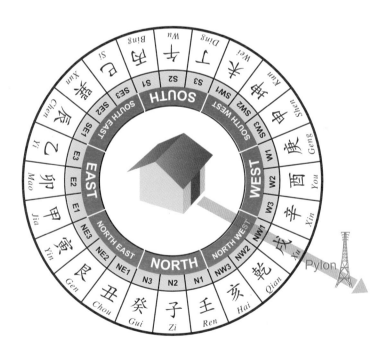

Pylons are a difficult problem to fix because of the size of the object and the fact that is is quite frankly, impossible to move. Sometimes, the strategic location of water can help reduce (the operative word is reduce, not eliminate) the impact of the pylon during certain years. This is because pylons are Fire element, and Water controls the intensity of the Fire element. Thus the strategic location of water can help but a proper consultation is needed to ensure the placement of water is correct. Nonetheless, living close to a pylon is not advisable, from both a Feng Shui and health perspective so it is best to pass up on a property that is close to a pylon.

THE INTERNAL ENVIRONMENT

227

Crack Between Buildings 天斬煞

In Feng Shui, this is known as Tian Zhan Sha 天斬煞 – Crack in the Sky Sha. This is caused by a gap between two buildings that are located very close together. When the wind blows through the gaps, it is focused and becomes sharp and piercing, creating very fierce Sha Qi. If this gap points right at your property, whichever sector it hits, will usually result in illness or injury associated with that Trigram.

Narrow gap between two buildings

So, for example, if the Sha hits Chen 辰 sector, then the occupants will get hurt in the legs, if it hits Gen 艮, as in the diagram below, then the occupants will experience back problem or sciatica.

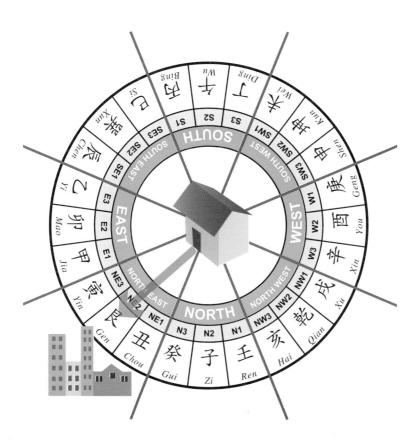

Curved Flyover 彎刀煞

This is known as Wan Dao Sha 彎刀煞 or Crescent Blade Sha. This Sha is also very intense and highly negative and it is one environmental feature that you must be on the look out for. Why is this Sha such a substantial cause for concern? Because it is near impossible to fix – unless you can somehow make the flyover bend in a different direction! If you have a choice, try to avoid choosing a house or an apartment unit near the curve or avoid being at the receiving end of the curve. If your property is located away from the curve, but within proximity of a flyover, it is okay. However, to be on the safe side, try to stay away from any property near curved flyovers.

Peeping Tom Sha 探頭峰

Imagine a person peeping up from behind a building – this is what Peeping Tom Sha (探頭峰– Tan Tou Feng) looks like. This formation is discussed in the ancient San He classics and refers to a mountain that peeps out from behind another mountain. It is a natural environmental formation, a combination of Zhen (3) and Dui (7) Gua. This combination should be avoided because it is known as a combination that produces thieves and causes robbery.

Peeping Tom

Natural mountains with the Tan Tao Feng 探頭峰

Natural mountains with the Tan Tao Feng 探頭峰

A Peeping Tom formation in an urban environment

Peeping Tom

Now, to the untrained eye, it is difficult to perceive, especially in a modern urban environment. But, these features do exist. If the Peeping Tom Sha hits a sector where there is also a 3-7 or 7-3 combo in the Flying Star chart, this denotes the occupants of the home will experience robbery, theft, fraud and embezzlement.

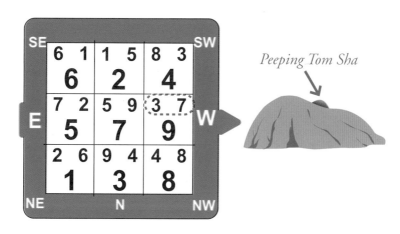

Peeping Tom Sha

THE INTERNAL ENVIRONMENT

233

White Tiger Sha 白虎煞

The term "White Tiger" refers to the right side of the property (looking out from the door). White Tiger Sha is present when there is a negative environmental feature on the right side of the property. This is especially strong Sha if the negative environmental feature is a sharp object, such as a sharp roof or pylons. The reason is that White Tiger is Metal element, whilst the sharp object is Fire element – Metal counters Fire in the study of the Five Elements. Accordingly, there is an antagonistic relationship between the elements in the immediate environment of the property. "White Tiger" relates to female matters and female power so White Tiger Sha usually causes imbalance to the female energies of the house. The women in the house will feel emotional, and will behave irrationally, causing problems for the household and the family.

Pylon on the right side of a property

Facing

The "White Tiger Opening Mouth" formation is present when there is a large arch or a sharp object within the arch, that is present on the right side of the property, when looking out from the Main Door. If you see such a formation, it denotes widows in the home or disputes between the women of the house and domestic problems for the man of the house.

House with wide, round opening on the right side

House Facing

Chapter Five:
What's not Feng Shui
- What is not of any
importance when
evaluating property

Having discussed everything of importance relating to your property's external Feng Shui, I thought it is essential to also inform you about what is not important and not of significance. In my many years of Feng Shui consulting, you will not believe the questions I have been asked, or the objects I have been shown which home owners believe to be the cause of negative Qi in their homes (or beneficial positive Qi). Occasionally, one does come across home owners who are positively paranoid just because of something they read, heard or saw on television.

This section has been written so that you can maximise the freedom you have in designing the home of your dreams and also, to help you avoid 'Feng Shui Paranoia'. The last few chapters have covered the dos and don'ts – this chapter will tell you what are the 'don't bother to get worked up about' scenarios that you don't have to lose sleep or sweat over when it comes to your home or a prospective property.

Types of Plants in your home

Plants and types of plants are usually quite harmless and have nothing to do with Classical Feng Shui. Plants are not mentioned in respect of Feng Shui in the ancient texts and really, what kind of plants you have in your home do not affect the Feng Shui of the property. A thousand money plants are not going to bring you more wealth, and planting Mother-In-Laws tongue is not going to give you mother-in-law problems. It's all in the name but nothing to do with Qi. And let me definitively put to death, once and for all, the myth that cactus emanates Sha Qi. It does not. Just because it has pointy needles does not mean it is directing Sha Qi at you or at your home.

The same goes with the auspicious plants, like peonies. Firstly, peonies only open once a season in China and are somewhat difficult to cultivate in any other part of the world. Having peonies in your garden does not mean your love life will get better, just as not having peonies in your home does not mean you have no romance in your life at all.

The key to remember with items like plants, figurines and furniture is that often, many Chinese things have flowery names or romantic sounding names, with meaning, but that does not mean it should be taken literally. If you like culturally-inspired furniture or even a Chinese style garden, then by all means, put one in. If you don't, you won't be losing out on any Qi!

The type of flower you have in your garden does not affect your Feng Shui

Paintings/décor

Some clients sweat over what type of paintings or deities they need to display. I recently saw in a magazine that said that waterfall paintings must flow in a certain directions, paintings must have sailing ships and all pond paintings must have 9 fishes for good Feng Shui. In fact, this just shows the misconceptions that people have about Feng Shui.

Paintings are a form of art, they are a form of expression, painting a lot of wealth does not make you rich. If that was the case, none of the great artists of the world would be rich because none of them paint dollar signs in their pictures. And honestly, let's just think about the implications of this idea. Does putting a wall poster of the movie 'Exorcist' mean your house will be haunted? Of course not.

Paintings are a positive and empowering motif but only if the art appeals to you on an aesthetic level. If it gives you pleasure to look at, then buy and place art in your home. Usually Chinese people like paintings with positive connotations for positive inspiration. When it comes to art, there are no rules on what you can have on the walls because it has nothing to do with Feng Shui. Remember, buy inspiration, not superstition.

Colour of roof/colour of walls

This is a great concern of many people and clients I have met. Some people believe if you have a blue roof, your house is underwater and the residents are drowning. This is very imaginative but purely symbolic and completely false in its interpretation. Many great buildings in the world have blue roofs – many of the Taiwanese government buildings have a blue roof – is the government drowning? The Temple of Heaven in China has a blue roof. Blue is the colour of the sky, could this be the reason why these ancient buildings had blue roofs? Symbolism is not Feng Shui. Have your roof any colour you want or most importantly, like.

The Temple of Heaven in China

In Asia, people are meticulous and sometimes, pointlessly so. To the extent that the size of the door and even the tables become an issue of contention. Now, there is such a thing as auspicious measurements in Feng Shui. In fact, you may even have heard of the Feng Shui ruler (no, I'm not kidding you).

But, specific auspicious measurements and the aforementioned ruler are usually used for the tombstone, coffin or for Yin House Feng Shui. Auspicious measurements are of greater significance when you are designing Feng Shui for a tomb. For Yang House, which is the Feng Shui term for property that has living occupants, it is not necessary to be so meticulous and whether or not your door and table has an auspicious measurement has no major effect on the occupants. You can safely ignore this issue.

Ba Gua mirrors

Should you buy a house facing a property that has a Ba Gua mirror? Or should you be worried about a property that has a Ba Gua mirror? The answer is no. The Ba Gua mirror's significance comes from the old days, when mirrors were made of brass and the objective was to introduce some metal into the sector. Ba Gua mirrors may have some significance in the spiritual practice fields, but in Feng Shui, it has no significance. Do not be afraid of a neighbour with a Ba Gua mirror or a house with a Ba Gua mirror (if you don't like it, just take it down!).

Isn't the Ba Gua a Feng Shui tool you may ask?
Sorry to disappoint you here but the "Ba Gua" is nothing more than a diagram indicating a mathematical model of the universe. In this model, the universe is based on the polarities of Yin (Negative) and Yang (Positive). By itself, the Ba Gua has no special 'powers'.

It is not uncommon to see the Ba Gua mirrors used for SPIRITUAL purposes – mostly after a host of prayers and rituals are done to them. They are used to ward off spirits in certain circumstances as well. But, this is not a Feng Shui practice. In Feng Shui, we only use the Ba Gua (without the mirror) as a diagram for calculations and to derive formulas.

Symbols like the Ba Gua mirror have power only in the minds of those who believe in them. The Ba Gua is akin to a country's flag. A flag inspires patriotism. But on its own, a flag is just a piece of coloured cloth with no special powers.

Stone lions (Fu Dogs)

Someone once told me that stone lions in the house are a great burglar deterrent. In all my years of research, I have never seen a Feng Shui classic that says this. Stone lions are just a Chinese decorative preference. The lions themselves do not generate any 'protective Qi' as it is made of ordinary stone. Will it scare off any thieves? Wishful thinking. The best way to prevent burglars? Install an alarm or get a real dog.

House number

This phobia about numbers having Feng Shui significance is something I've written extensively about in my book, Stories and Lessons on Feng Shui. Suffice to say, there is no Feng Shui curse if you happen to be on the 14th floor or house number 14. Hey, don't discount the property just because of the number. If house number 14 has great Feng Shui, why not live there? Similarly, house number 8 may have an auspicious sounding number, but that auspicious number 8 is not going to help you if you have a negative feature outside your Main Door or insulate you against the effects of a busy T-junction. Chinese people like things to have meaningful names, but remember, we're talking about Qi in the environment here and it has nothing to do with your house number.

Garden/landscape Feng Shui

Garden Feng Shui apparently is the latest thing to sweep the world. Landscaping pathways, plants and trees apparently can make a difference to your Feng Shui and the Qi in your property.

The pathways, footways, plants and trees generally do not make any difference to the Qi surrounding your property. Of course, due consideration must be given to any external water or bodies of water such as ponds created by landscaping or rock gardens or rock waterfalls.

Patio

You do not live on the patio or sleep there at night. Therefore, it is not an important consideration for Feng Shui! Yes, it is that simple. You can locate it where you like in your property.

Pergola

This is a sort of outdoor gazebo that is common and popular in
the west. As long as the edges of the roof do not point at your
Main Door, the location of the pergola is not important.

Garden lamp posts

Many people are overly concerned about the number of bulbs in the garden lamp post – no, there is no significance in five bulbs, eight bulbs or ten! Remember, we are concerned with the positioning or location, not the symbolism. Garden lamp posts are generally not dangerous as long as they are not directly in front of any of the doors to your property.

Many people spend a lot of money buying crystal chandeliers believing that the lead crystals are able to disperse beautiful Qi around the property. The crystals do not emit any Qi but they emit beautiful light. Chose the crystal chandelier because you like it, not because you are looking to get more Qi (you won't get any!).

Chapter Six:
How to Screen
a House

We've come a long way since Chapter 1. By this point, you are familiar with the concepts of Sheng Qi and Sha Qi in the environment. You know how to identify some basic Sheng Qi and Sha Qi forms. You've probably even started to identify some landforms in the area that you are presently living in. Slowly but surely, you are getting the idea of looking at the environment with 'Feng Shui Vision'.

In this chapter, I am going to walk you through the process of screening a house, using the information that has been given to you in the preceding chapters. Now, while this mimics what most Classical Feng Shui practitioners will do when they audit a property, remember that you are not auditing the place like a Feng Shui consultant would, but screening. So your goal should be to evaluate the environment as best as you can, placing priority on certain environmental features such as mountains and water.

So, assuming your real estate agent has called you to inform you of the availability of a house or property that suits your interests or budget, whatever your consideration may be. What is the first step in screening this property to evaluate its Feng Shui Quotient (FSQ)?

Assuming you have a basic compass or an electronic compass, then the next step is to get hold of a map of the area. This will make identifying the location of rivers and mountains in the vicinity of your home a lot easier. If you want to be high tech about it, you may want to try your local city map. I use it a lot in my practice and it's great for getting an overview perspective of a neighbourhood.

Joey Yap's Mini Feng Shui Compass

The map helps not only to identify the mountains and rivers in the vicinity but also to give you an idea of their directional location, in relation to your house. Sometimes, from the property itself, especially in an urban landscape, the mountains and rivers may not be visible. So the map helps you know where they are in advance.

Joey Yap's Mini Feng Shui Compass

Step #2: Drive around the area

Armed with your map, you should now take a drive around the area. Drive around, several times, in front, behind and in a circuit around the neighbourhood – it's best to have someone do the driving because spotting mountains and rivers while driving can be dangerous! The idea here is to try to get an idea of where the mountains and rivers are located in proximity and orientation to your house (for example, are they on the right, left, front or back of the property) but also to look around for any major environmental forms such as sharp roofs, or highways or LRT lines that will not show up on your map. Make a note of where these features are located on your map. At this juncture, you should be concerned with 'big' forms like buildings or major highways. Remember, you need to always relate these forms that you observe back to the property you are considering. The focal point is the property that you are considering.

Basically, if the little excursion shows no mountains, hills or rivers in the vicinity of up to a 10km radius, you may seriously want to reconsider buying property in this neighbourhood. Remember, Mountains or hills are the carriers of Qi and if you have no mountains in the area, then the Qi in the area is probably weak or stagnant. You certainly don't want to tap into stagnant or weak Qi for well-being and personal prosperity.

Now, there is of course the principle of 'Flat Land Dragon' (Ping Yang Long 平洋龍) that Feng Shui practitioners use for absolutely flat land but this is a very sophisticated concept that requires a lot of skill to utilise and a sharp keen eye to determine if the land is truly flat. As a very general rule, for screening purposes, if there are no mountains, or even low hills within a 10km radius of the property, you'd be wise to pass up on that purchase.

Check for hills and lakes in the vicinity

Assuming you do find mountains and hills in the vicinity, you need to do one more check. Have a good look at these mountains – are they Sheng Long 生龍 or Healthy Dragons or are they Bing Long 病龍 or Sick Dragons? Now, you might be wondering how you can tell. Well, most of us can tell what a sick person looks like right? They have a sickly parlour, their skin looks pale, they look down and wrung out. A Sick Dragon is usually a bony harsh and dried out looking mountain. The rock is exposed and sharp. By contrast, a Healthy Dragon is a mountain in the 'green' of health. It is lush, green and nurturing. It's the kind of place that you'd think about having a picnic next to!

Assuming you have mountains and rivers in the vicinity, then you can safely move on to the next step, which is to evaluate the impact of any negative features in the environment.

Sick Dragon

Healthy Dragon

Now, we're not done with the exterior yet. Once you have checked the immediate environment, it's time to take a look at your Qi container, the house. First, get a plan of the house, preferably one that shows you the actual plot of land. You will need this to look at the shape of the land.

A plan of the property will enable you to check whether or not the shape of the land gives rise to any obvious problems, such as in-built Sha Qi or a missing sector problem. Remember, we like square land the best and we want to avoid odd or unusual shapes. If you are looking at land without a property built on it, remember to check the soil and make sure it's not muddy or rocky land or any of the types of land that make for bad Qi containers.

Assuming the land is fine, then you need to observe the house itself. Make sure that you don't have any imbalanced or uneven features in the roof or façade.

Step #5: The House Plan

Assuming your land passes the test, meaning, you know it is capable of collecting and storing Qi, then it's time to evaluate the impact of any negative environmental features in the area. The objective at this stage is to make sure that the house is not affected by any negative or Sha Qi. For this, you will need a house plan.

The reason why we need the house plan is so that you can use the handy stencil provided at the start of this book to help you get the 8 directions using the pie division method.

Mark out the 8 cardinal directions, based on the Facing of your house. So for example, if your house faces West, your house plan, with the 8 directions marked in, will look something like the diagram below.

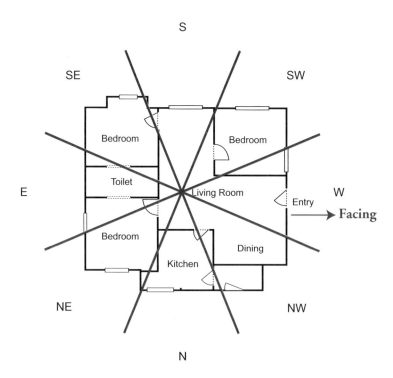

You'll notice that the lines marking the directions have been deliberately extended beyond the boundaries of the house plan. This is so that you can use the same plan to determine the location of any positive or negative landforms and environmental features.

Once you have done this, it is time to fit in the information that you have obtained from the map and from your drive around the neighbourhood. So for example, if you have observed a sharp roof or negative environmental feature in the South, then note that down on your house plan. If you have a mountain in the East, then mark that down. Perhaps you know the river runs through the North sector of your house – make a note of that. In the end, you should end up with a diagram like below.

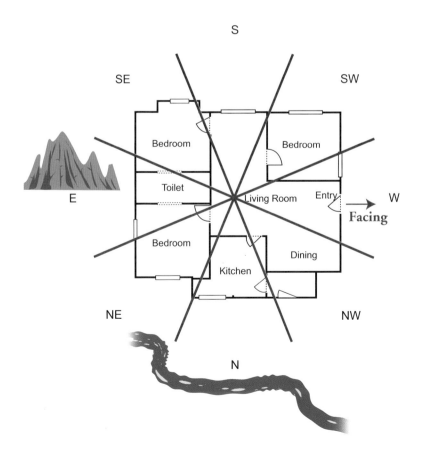

Remember, don't panic just because you find a few negative environmental features in the area. Feng Shui is not paranoia remember? Also, remember that finding the perfect house is not an easy task and you should be prepared for a few 'warts' in the neighbourhood. The presence of negative features are not a big deal if they do not affect you or any of the occupants in your house adversely or if perhaps you have a positive environmental feature or landform that helps suppress the negative impact of the negative feature or the Sha Qi.

If you find a Sha Qi in the South sector of the property for example, but you do not have a Li Gua or a middle aged woman person living in your home, then no big deal. Check each of the sectors and the negative features against the Trigram attributes. Assuming that you find the negative features present in the area do not affect any of the occupants, you can proceed to the next stage of checking the interior features of the house, safe in the knowledge that you have at the very least, this property is located in a good environment.

After the Exterior, What Next?

If you have checked the exterior environment and are satisfied that the property is in an area that receives Qi from the mountains, is a good container of Qi and is not being struck by or affected by negative Qi, you can then look into the interior of the house and determine if the house has positive and favourable attributes that enhance its basic good Feng Shui Quotient. What we are looking for in the interior is a layout, set-up and location of key features such as the Main Door, bedroom and kitchen, as well as study, that taps into all the positive Qi in the environment and circulates the Qi around the house so all the inhabitants can benefit from it.

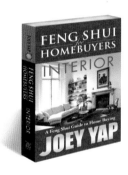

Interior Feng Shui, while secondary to the landform in the environment, represents a fine-tuning of the house, through the use and placement of the various rooms and the individual inhabitants. So it is an important consideration. However, many people make the mistake of prioritising the interior, without looking at the exterior. I hope that this book has been able to correct that perception and provide you with the right set of tools and the knowledge you need, to judge the environment first. Evaluating a house from the inside, looking at issues such as the Main Door, and interior forms, is covered in my next book, *Feng Shui for Homebuyers: Interior*.

Do not be disheartened if you find a property of your dreams has a few Feng Shui warts so to speak. Few houses are absolutely perfect. But remember, at all times, that your goal is not perfection, but a house with a good Feng Shui Quotient (FSQ)

– a property that is located in an area with good Qi, that is built to receive and attract Qi rather than repel it, and is located in an area with a minimum of negative features or Sha Qi. Achieving this is very do-able and perfectly within the capabilities of anyone, as long as they have a compass and are prepared to do some homework!

Familiarise yourself with the various environmental features and landforms discussed in this book, do a little simple legwork and preparation and you would have done a lot to give yourself an advantage in life by ensuring you have a property with a good Feng Shui Quotient (FSQ). And that is truly the best start you can give to yourself.

Happy House Hunting!

24 Mountain Stencil

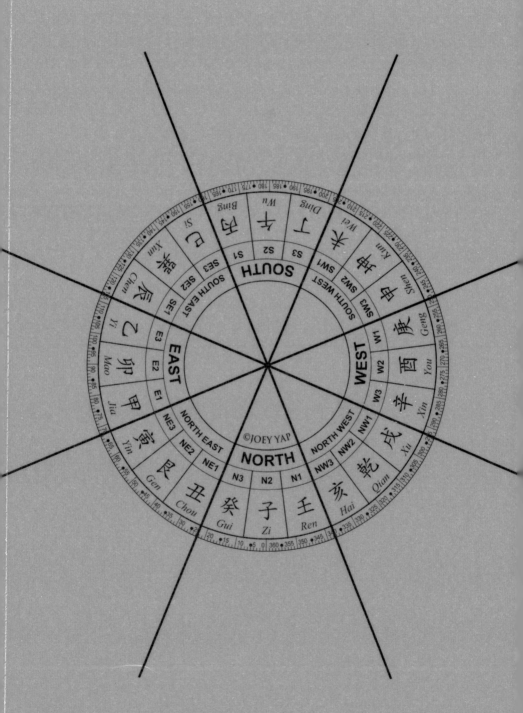

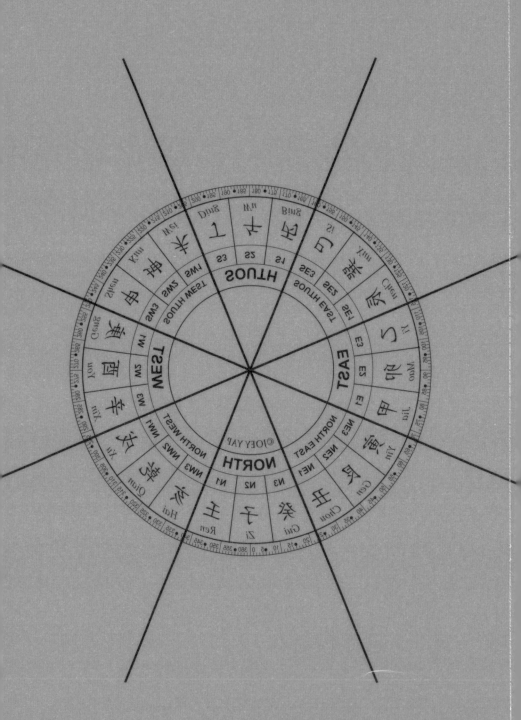

About Joey Yap

Joey Yap is the founder and Master Trainer of the Mastery Academy of Chinese Metaphysics, a global organisation devoted to the worldwide teaching of Feng Shui, BaZi, Mian Xiang and other Chinese Metaphysics subjects. Joey is also the CEO of Yap Global Consulting, a Feng Shui and Chinese Astrology consulting firm offering audit and consultation services to corporations and individuals all over the world.

Joey received his formal education in Malaysia and Australia. He has combined the best of Eastern learning and Western education systems in the teaching methodology practiced at the Academy. Students of the Mastery Academy study traditional syllabuses of Chinese Metaphysics but through Western-style modular programs that are structured and systematic, enabling individuals to easily and quickly learn, grasp and master complex Chinese Metaphysics subjects like Feng Shui and BaZi. These unique structured learning systems are also utilized by Mastery Academy instructors all over the world to teach BaZi and Feng Shui.

The Mastery Academy is also the first international educational organisation to fully utilize the benefits of the Internet to promote continuous education, encourage peer-to-peer learning, enable mentoring and distance learning. Students interact with each other live, and continue to learn and improve their knowledge.

Despite his busy schedule, Joey continues to write for the Mastery Journal, a monthly eZine on Feng Shui and Astrology devoted for world-wide readers and the production of the world's first bilingual "Ten Thousand Year Calendar". He is also the best selling author of "Stories and Lessons on Feng Shui", "Mian Xiang- Discover Face Reading", "Tong Shu Diary" and "BaZi - The Destiny Code". Besides being a regular guest of various radio and TV talk shows, Joey is also a regular columnist for a national newspaper and various magazines in Malaysia, as well as being the host of "*Discover Feng Shui with Joey Yap*" on national 8TV Channel, a popular program which focused on education in Feng Shui and Chinese Metaphysics studies.

Author's personal website: www.joeyyap.com
Academy website: www.masteryacademy.com I www.masteryjournal.com

EDUCATION
The Mastery Academy of Chinese Metaphysics: the first choice for practitioners and aspiring students of the art and science of Chinese Classical Feng Shui and Astrology.

For thousands of years, Eastern knowledge has been passed from one generation to another through the system of discipleship. A venerated Master would accept suitable individuals at a young age as his disciples, and informally through the years, pass on his knowledge and skills to them. His disciples in turn, would take on their own disciples, as a means to perpetuate knowledge or skills.

This system served the purpose of restricting the transfer of knowledge to only worthy honourable individuals and ensuring that outsiders or Westerners would not have access to thousands of years of Eastern knowledge, learning and research.

However, the disciple system has also resulted in Chinese Metaphysics and Classical Studies lacking systematic teaching methods. Knowledge garnered over the years has not been accumulated in a concise, systematic manner, but scattered amongst practitioners, each practicing his/her knowledge, art and science, in isolation.

The disciple system, out of place in today's modern world, endangers the advancement of these classical fields that continue to have great relevance and application today.

At the Mastery Academy of Chinese Metaphysics, our Mission is to bring Eastern Classical knowledge in the fields of metaphysics, Feng Shui and Astrology sciences and the arts to the world. These Classical teachings and knowledge, previously shrouded in secrecy and passed on only through the discipleship system, are adapted into structured learning, which can easily be understood, learnt and mastered. Through modern learning methods, these renowned ancient arts, sciences and practices can be perpetuated while facilitating more extensive application and understanding of these classical subjects.

The Mastery Academy espouses an educational philosophy that draws from the best of the East and West . It is the world's premier educational institution for the study of Chinese Metaphysics Studies offering a wide range and variety of courses, ensuring that students have the opportunity to pursue their preferred field of study and enabling existing practitioners and professionals to gain cross-disciplinary knowledge that complements their current field of practice.

Courses at the Mastery Academy have been carefully designed to ensure a comprehensive yet compact syllabus. The modular nature of the courses enables students to immediately begin to put their knowledge into practice while pursuing continued study of their field and complimentary fields. Students thus have the benefit of developing and gaining practical experience in tandem with the expansion and advancement of their theoretical knowledge.

Students can also choose from a variety of study options, from a distance learning program, the Homestudy Series, that enables study at one's own pace or intensive foundation courses and compact lecture-based courses, held in various cities around the world by Joey Yap or our licensed instructors. The Mastery Academy's faculty and make-up is international in nature, thus ensuring that prospective students can attend courses at destinations nearest to their country of origin or with a licensed Mastery Academy instructor in their home country.

The Mastery Academy provides 24x7 support to students through its Online Community, with a variety of tools, documents, forums and e-learning materials to help students stay at the forefront of research in their fields and gain invaluable assistance from peers and mentoring from their instructors.

TM

MASTERY ACADEMY
OF CHINESE METAPHYSICS

www.masteryacademy.com

19-3, The Boulevard, Mid Valley City,
59200 Kuala Lumpur, Malaysia.
Tel: +603-2284 8080, +603-2284 8318
Fax: +603-2284 1218
Email: info@masteryacademy.com
Website: www.masteryacademy.com

Represented In:
Australia, Austria, Brazil, Canada, China, Cyprus, France, Germany, Greece, Hungary, India, Japan, Indonesia, Italy, Malaysia, Mexico, Netherlands, New Zealand, Philippines, Russian Federation, Poland, Singapore, South Africa, Switzerland, Turkey, U.S.A., Ukraine, United Kingdom

Mastery Academy around the world

Canada

United States

Mexico

Brazil

United Kingdom
Switzerland
Netherlands
France
Austria
Poland
Germany
Italy
Cyprus
Hungary
Greece

Russian
Federation

Ukraine

Turkey

India

South Africa

China

Japan

Philippines
Kuala Lumpur
Malaysia

Indonesia

Singapore

Australia

New Zealand

YAP GLOBAL CONSULTING SDN. BHD.

- Feng Shui Estate Design and Planning • Land Selection • Feng Shui for Residences • Feng Shui for Offices • Feng Shui for Corporate Headquarters • Feng Shui for Commercial Properties • Date Selection for Official Openings & Business Transactions • Date Selection for Individuals • BaZi/ Destiny Analysis for Corporations • BaZi/Destiny Analysis for Individuals • BaZi/Destiny Analysis for Career • BaZi/Destiny Analysis for Relationships • Corporate Seminars • Private Seminars • Public Talks

Yap Global Consulting is the foremost international Feng Shui and BaZi consulting firm, offering professional confidential consultations and audits for individuals and corporations. We benchmark our services against the standards of international consulting firms, bringing a distinctly professional approach to BaZi/Destiny Analysis and Feng Shui auditing and consulting.

Yap Global Consulting's CEO and Principal Consultant, Mr. Joey Yap, is a Master Trainer for the Mastery Academy of Chinese Metaphysics, the world's first learning organisation dedicated to the study of Chinese Metaphysics. Our global reach is supported by an international team of professional and highly experienced Senior Consultants. No matter where you are located in the world, Yap Global Consulting has experienced and professional consultants available to conduct BaZi consultations and Feng Shui audits and consultations for you.

For more details or to make an appointment,
visit www.joeyyap.com or contact us at:

Tel   : +603-2284 1213
Fax   : +603-2284 2213
Email : consultations@joeyyap.com

Or you may visit our office by appointment at

19-3, The Boulevard,
Mid Valley City,
59200 Kuala Lumpur, Malaysia.

www.joeyyap.com

Feng Shui for Homebuyers Series

Feng Shui For Homebuyers (Exterior)

Best selling author and international Feng Shui consultant, Joey Yap will guide you on the various important features in your external environment that have a bearing on the Feng Shui of your home. A book that will benefit homeowners, those looking to build their own home or even investors who are looking to apply Feng Shui to their homes, this book provides valuable information from the classical Feng Shui theories and applications.

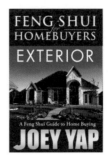

This book will assist you in screening and eliminating unsuitable options with negative FSQ (Feng Shui Quotient) should you acquire your own land or if you are purchasing a newly built home. This book will also help you in determining which plot of land to select and which are best avoided when purchasing an empty parcel of land.

Feng Shui for Homebuyers (Interior)

A book every homeowner or potential house buyer should have. The Feng Shui for Homebuyers (Interior) is an informative reference book and invaluable guide written by best selling author and international Feng Shui consultant, Joey Yap.

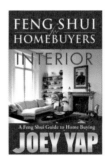

This book provides answers to the important questions of what really does matter when looking at the internal Feng Shui of a home or office. It teaches you how to analyze your home or office floor plans and how to improve the Feng Shui. It will answer all your questions about the positive and negative flow of Qi within your home and ways to utilize them to your maximum benefit.

Providing you with a guide to calculating your Life Gua and House Gua to fine-tune your Feng Shui within your property, Joey Yap focuses on practical, easily applicable ideas on what you can implement internally in a property.

Check Your Property's Feng Shui With Joey Yap's Mini Feng Shui Compass

Mini Feng Shui Compass

This Mini Feng Shui Compass with the accompanying Companion Booklet written by leading Feng Shui and Chinese Astrology Master Trainer Joey Yap is a must-have for any Feng Shui enthusiast.

The Mini Feng Shui Compass is a self-aligning compass that is not only light at 100gms but also built sturdily to ensure it will be convenient to use anywhere. The rings on the Mini Feng Shui Compass are bi-lingual and incorporate the 24 Mountains rings that is used in your traditional Luo Pan.

A comprehensive booklet included will guide you in applying the 24 Mountain Directions on your Mini Feng Shui Compass effectively and the 8 Mansions Feng Shui to locate the most auspicious locations within your home, office and surroundings. You can also use the Mini Feng Shui Compass when measuring the direction of your property for the purpose of applying Flying Stars Feng Shui.

Accelerate Your Face Reading Skills With Joey Yap's Face Reading Revealed DVD Series

Face Reading Revealed – DVD 1
Introduction to Face Reading

Mian Xiang, the Chinese art of Face Reading is an ancient form of physiognomy and entails the use of the face and facial characteristics to evaluate key aspects of a person's life, luck and destiny. In this Introduction to Face Reading DVD, Joey Yap shows you how the eyes, ears, mouth, nose and eyebrows reveal a wealth of information about a person's luck, destiny and personality.

Face Reading Revealed – DVD 2
12 Palaces of the Face

Mian Xiang reveals not just a person's destiny and fortune, but talents, quirks and personality. Did you know that just by looking at a person's face, you can ascertain a wealth of information about their health, wealth, relationships and career? In this DVD, Joey Yap shows you how the 12 Palaces can be utilised to reveal a person's inner talents, personality quirks and much more.

Face Reading Revealed – DVD 3
100 Positions of the Face - Ages 1 to 30

Each facial feature on the face represents one year in a person's life. Joey Yap guides you through the 100 year map of the face and shares with you which features on your face govern your luck between the ages of 1 to 30. Also, learn how to deploy Fixed Position Face Reading and Multiple Position Face Reading techniques in this lively, entertaining and educational DVD.

Accelerate Your Face Reading Skills With Joey Yap's Face Reading Revealed DVD Series

Face Reading Revealed – DVD 4
100 Positions of the Face
- Ages 31 to 100

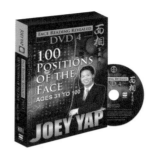

Your face is a 100 year map of your life but each position not only reveals your fortune and destiny for that age, but also reveals insights and information about your personality, skills, abilities and destiny. Delve deeper into the 100 year map of the face and discover, with Joey Yap, what facial features determine your luck between the ages of 31-100.

Face Reading Revealed – DVD 5
How to Read Face Shapes

This highly entertaining and insightful DVD shows you how just by evaluating the shape of a person's face, you can learn about their abilities, inclinations, personality and capacity in life. What does a Water face person excel in? What is the personality of a Metal faced person? Let Joey Yap show you the differences between the 10 character faces and how to discern the 5 basic element face shapes in this fun, entertaining and educational DVD.

Face Reading Revealed – DVD 6
The Significance of Moles, Hair and Birthmarks

Do moles have meanings? Yes, they do and in Face Reading, moles, birthmarks and even the type of hair on your head can reveal a lot about a person. Find out the meaning of moles on the face, what kinds of moles are favourable and unfavourable and whether or not you should remove certain moles with Feng Shui, Chinese Astrology and Face Reading Master Trainer Joey Yap.

Continue Your Journey with Joey Yap's Books

The Ten Thousand Year Calendar

The Ten Thousand Year Calendar or 萬年曆 Wan Nian Li is a regular reference book and an invaluable tool used by masters, practitioners and students of Feng Shui, BaZi (Four Pillars of Destiny), Chinese Zi Wei Dou Shu Astrology (Purple Star), Yi Jing (I-Ching) and Date Selection specialists.

JOEY YAP's Ten Thousand Year Calendar provides the Gregorian (Western) dates converted into both the Chinese Solar and Lunar calendar in both the English and Chinese language.

It also includes a comprehensive set of key Feng Shui and Chinese Astrology charts and references, including Xuan Kong Nine Palace Flying Star Charts, Monthly and Daily Flying Stars, Water Dragon Formulas Reference Charts, Zi Wei Dou Shu (Purple Star) Astrology Reference Charts, BaZi (Four Pillars of Destiny) Heavenly Stems, Earthly Branches and all other related reference tables for Chinese Metaphysical Studies.

Stories and Lessons on Feng Shui

Stories and Lessons on Feng Shui is a compilation of essays and stories written by leading Feng Shui and Chinese Astrology trainer and consultant Joey Yap about Feng Shui and Chinese Astrology.

In this heart-warming collection of easy to read stories, find out why it's a myth that you should never have Water on the right hand side of your house, the truth behind the infamous 'love' and 'wealth' corners and that the sudden death of a pet fish is really NOT due to bad luck!

BaZi - The Destiny Code

Leading Chinese Astrology Master Trainer Joey Yap makes it easy to learn how to unlock your Destiny through your BaZi with this book. BaZi or Four Pillars of Destiny is an ancient Chinese science which enables individuals to understand their personality, hidden talents and abilities as well as their luck cycle, simply by examining the information contained within their birth data. The Destiny Code is the first book that shows readers how to plot and interpret their own Destiny Charts and lays the foundation for more in-depth BaZi studies. Written in a lively entertaining style, the Destiny Code makes BaZi accessible to the layperson. Within 10 chapters, understand and appreciate more about this astoundingly accurate ancient Chinese Metaphysical science.

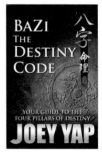

Continue Your Journey with Joey Yap's Books

Mian Xiang - Discover Face Reading

Need to identify a suitable business partner? How about understanding your staff or superiors better? Or even choosing a suitable spouse? These mind boggling questions can be answered in Joey Yap's introductory book to Face Reading titled 'Mian Xiang – Discover Face Reading'. This book will help you discover the hidden secrets in a person's face.

Mian Xiang – Discover Face Reading is comprehensive book on all areas of Face Reading, covering some of the most important facial features, including the forehead, mouth, ears and even the philtrum above your lips. This book will help you analyse not just your Destiny but help you achieve your full potential and achieve life fulfillment.

Xuan Kong - Flying Stars Feng Shui

Xuan Kong Flying Stars Feng Shui is an essential introductory book to the subject of Xuan Kong Fei Xing, a well-known and popular system of Feng Shui, written by the International Feng Shui Master Trainer Joey Yap.

In his down-to-earth, entertaining and easy to read style, Joey Yap takes you through the essential basics of Classical Feng Shui, and the key concepts of Xuan Kong Fei Xing (Flying Stars). Learn how to fly the stars, plot a Flying Star chart for your home or office and interpret the stars and star combinations. Find out how to utilise the favourable areas of your home or office for maximum benefit and learn 'tricks of the trade' and 'trade secrets' used by Feng Shui practitioners to enhance and maximise Qi in your home or office.

An essential integral introduction to the subject of Classical Feng Shui and the Flying Stars System of Feng Shui.

Feng Shui and Astrology for 2006

The Annual influences of each year play a crucial role in determining the Feng Shui of your property as well as your Destiny for the year 2006. Learn all about what 2006 holds in store for you with best selling author Joey Yap's new book - Feng Shui & Astrology for 2006.

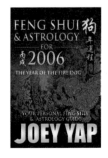

This book will reveal the Feng Shui path ahead by charting out the Annual and Monthly Flying Stars, and explaining the influence the various sectors have on the occupants of the property. Based on your Chinese Zodiac animal sign, you will also be able to plan ahead using the Astrological guide for the year.

Discover the monthly guide to the Feng Shui of your home and learn how to manage it on a monthly basis as Joey Yap guides you with a clear explanation on what the effects will be and what you can do to mitigate them. Date selection is also a breeze with the auspicious dates for important activities already pre-selected in this book.

Elevate Your Feng Shui Skills With Joey Yap's Home Study Course And Educational DVDs

Xuan Kong Vol.1
An Advanced Feng Shui Home Study Course

Learn the Xuan Kong Flying Star Feng Shui system in just 20 lessons! Joey Yap's specialised notes and course work have been written to enable distance learning without compromising on the breadth or quality of the syllabus. Learn at your own pace and learn the same material students in a live class would learn. The most comprehensive distance learning course on Xuan Kong Flying Star Feng Shui in the market. Xuan Kong Flying Star Vol. 1 comes complete with a special binder for all your course notes.

Feng Shui for Period 8 - (DVD)

Don't miss the Feng Shui Event of the next 20 years! Catch Joey Yap LIVE and find out just what Period 8 is all about. This DVD boxed set zips you through the fundamentals of Feng Shui and the impact of this important change in the Feng Shui calendar. Joey's entertaining, conversational style walks you through the key changes that Period 8 will bring and how to tap into Wealth Qi and Good Feng Shui for the next 20 years.

Xuan Kong Flying Stars Beginners Workshop - (DVD)

Take a front row seat in Joey Yap's Xuan Kong Flying Stars workshop with this unique LIVE RECORDING of Joey Yap's Xuan Kong Flying Stars Feng Shui workshop, attended by over 500 people. This DVD program is an effective and quick introduction of Xuan Kong Feng Shui essentials for those who are just starting out in their study of classical Feng Shui. Learn to plot your own Flying Star chart in just 3 hours. Learn 'trade secret' methods, remedies and cures for Flying Stars Feng Shui. This boxed set contains 3 DVDs and 1 workbook with notes and charts for reference.

BaZi Four Pillars of Destiny Beginners Workshop - (DVD)

Ever wondered what Destiny has in store for you? Or curious to know how you can learn more about your personality and inner talents? BaZi or Four Pillars of Destiny is an ancient Chinese science that enables us to understand a person's hidden talent, inner potential, personality, health and wealth luck from just their birth data. This specially compiled DVD set of Joey Yap's BaZi Beginners Workshop provides a thorough and comprehensive introduction to BaZi. Learn how to read your own chart and understand your own luck cycle. This boxed set contains 3 DVDs, 1 workbook with notes and reference charts.

Interested in learning MORE about Feng Shui? Advance Your Feng Shui Knowledge with the Mastery Academy Courses.

Feng Shui Mastery Series™
™ LIVE COURSES (MODULES ONE TO FOUR)

Feng Shui Mastery – Module One
Beginners Course

Designed for students seeking an entry-level intensive program into the study of Feng Shui , Module One is an intensive foundation course that aims not only to provide you with an introduction to Feng Shui theories and formulas and equip you with the skills and judgments to begin practicing and conduct simple Feng Shui audits upon successful completion of the course. Learn all about Forms, Eight Mansions Feng Shui and Flying Star Feng Shui in just one day with a unique, structured learning program that makes learning Feng Shui quick and easy!

Feng Shui Mastery – Module Two
Practitioners Course

Building on the knowledge and foundation in classical Feng Shui theory garnered in M1, M2 provides a more advanced and in-depth understanding of Eight Mansions, Xuan Kong Flying Star and San He and introduces students to theories that are found only in the classical Chinese Feng Shui texts. This 3-Day Intensive course hones analytical and judgment skills, refines Luo Pan (Chinese Feng Shui compass) skills and reveals 'trade secret' remedies. Module Two covers advanced Forms Analysis, San He's Five Ghost Carry Treasure formula, Advanced Eight Mansions and Xuan Kong Flying Stars and equips you with the skills needed to undertake audits and consultations for residences and offices.

Feng Shui Mastery – Module Three
Advanced Practitioners Course

Module Three is designed for Professional Feng Shui Practitioners. Learn advanced topics in Feng Shui and take your skills to a cutting edge level. Be equipped with the knowledge, techniques and confidence to conduct large scale audits (like estate and resort planning). Learn how to apply different systems appropriately to remedy situations or cases deemed inauspicious by one system and reconcile conflicts in different systems of Feng Shui. Gain advanced knowledge of San He (Three Harmony) systems and San Yuan (Three Cycles) systems, advanced Luan Tou (Forms Feng Shui) and specialist Water Formulas.

Feng Shui Mastery – Module Four
Master Course

The graduating course of the Feng Shui Mastery (FSM) Series, this course takes the advanced practitioner to the Master level. Power packed M4 trains students to 'walk the mountains' and identify superior landform, superior grade structures and make qualitative evaluations of landform, structures, Water and Qi and covers advanced and exclusive topics of San He, San Yuan, Xuan Kong, Ba Zhai, Luan Tou (Advanced Forms and Water Formula) Feng Shui. Master Internal, External and Luan Tou (Landform) Feng Shui methodologies to apply Feng Shui at every level and undertake consultations of every scale and magnitude, from houses and apartments to housing estates, townships, shopping malls and commercial districts.

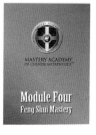

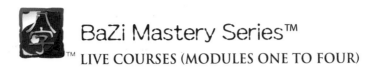

BaZi Mastery Series™
LIVE COURSES (MODULES ONE TO FOUR)

BaZi Mastery – Module One
Intensive Foundation Course

This Intensive One Day Foundation Course provides an introduction to the principles and fundamentals of BaZi (Four Pillars of Destiny) and Destiny Analysis methods such as Ten Gods, Useful God and Strength of Qi. Learn how to plot a BaZi chart and interpret your Destiny and your potential. Master BaZi and learn to capitalize on your strengths, minimize risks and downturns and take charge of your Destiny.

BaZi Mastery – Module Two
Practical BaZi Applications

BaZi Module Two teaches students advanced BaZi analysis techniques and specific analysis methods for relationship luck, health evaluation, wealth potential and career potential. Students will learn to identify BaZi chart structures, sophisticated methods for applying the Ten Gods, and how to read Auxiliary Stars. Students who have completed Module Two will be able to conduct professional BaZi readings.

BaZi Mastery – Module Three
Advanced Practitioners Program

Designed for the BaZi practitioner, learn how to read complex cases and unique events in BaZi charts and perform Big and Small assessments. Discover how to analyze personalities and evaluate talents precisely, as well as special formulas and classical methodologies for BaZi from classics such as Di Tian Sui and Qiong Tong Bao Jian.

BaZi Mastery – Module Four
Master Course in BaZi

The graduating course of the BaZi Mastery Series, this course takes the advanced practitioner to the Masters' level. BaZi M4 focuses on specialized techniques of BaZi reading, unique special structures and advance methods from ancient classical texts. This program includes techniques on date selection and ancient methodologies from the Qiong Tong Bao Jian and Yuan Hai Zi Ping classics.

XUAN KONG MASTERY SERIES™
LIVE COURSES (MODULES ONE TO THREE)
* Advanced Courses For Master Practitioners

Xuan Kong Mastery – Module One
Advanced Foundation Program

This course is for the experienced Feng Shui professionals who wish to expand their knowledge and skills in the Xuan Kong system of Feng Shui, covering important foundation methods and techniques from the Wu Chang and Guang Dong lineages of Xuan Kong Feng Shui.

Xuan Kong Mastery – Module Two A
Advanced Xuan Kong Methodologies

Designed for Feng Shui practitioners seeking to specialise in the Xuan Kong system, this program focuses on methods of application and Joey Yap's unique Life Palace and Shifting Palace Methods, as well as methods and techniques from the Wu Chang lineage.

Xuan Kong Mastery – Module Two B
Purple White

Explore in detail and in great depth the star combinations in Xuan Kong. Learn how each different combination reacts or responds in different palaces, under different environmental circumstances and to whom in the property. Learn methods, theories and techniques extracted from ancient classics such as Xuan Kong Mi Zhi, Xuan Kong Fu, Fei Xing Fu and Zi Bai Jue.

Xuan Kong Mastery – Module Three
Advanced Xuan Kong Da Gua

This intensive course focuses solely on the Xuan Kong Da Gua system covering the theories, techniques and methods of application of this unique 64-Hexagram based system of Xuan Kong including Xuan Kong Da Gua for landform analysis.

MIAN XIANG MASTERY SERIES™
™ LIVE COURSES (MODULES ONE AND TWO)

Mian Xiang Mastery – Module One
Basic Face Reading

A person's face is their fortune – learn more about the ancient Chinese art of Face Reading. In just one day, be equipped with techniques and skills to read a person's face and ascertain their character, luck, wealth and relationship luck.

Mian Xiang Mastery – Module Two
Practical Face Reading

Mian Xiang Module Two covers face reading techniques extracted from the ancient classics Shen Xiang Quan Pian and Shen Xiang Tie Guan Dau. Gain a greater depth and understanding of Mian Xiang and learn to recognize key structures and characteristics in a person's face.

Walking the Mountains! Learn Feng Shui in a Practical and Hands-on Program.

 Feng Shui Mastery Excursion Series™ : **CHINA**

Learn landform (Luan Tou) Feng Shui by walking the mountains and chasing the dragon's vein in China. This Program takes the students in a study tour to examine notable Feng Shui landmarks, mountains, hills, valleys, ancient palaces, famous mansions, houses and tombs in China. The Excursion is a 'practical' hands-on course where students are shown to perform readings using the formulas they've learnt and to recognize and read Feng Shui Landform (Luan Tou) formations.

Read about China Excursion here:
http://www.masteryacademy.com/Education/schoolfengshui/fengshuimasteryexcursion.asp

Mastery Academy courses are conducted around the world. Find out when will Joey Yap be in your area by visiting **www.masteryacademy.com** or call our office at +603-2284 8080 or +603-2284 8318.